Y0-BCR-401

SCHOLASTIC

Grades 5 & Up

Note Taking Made Easy!

Strategies & Scaffolded Lessons
for Helping All Students Take Effective Notes,
Summarize, and Learn the Content They Need to Know

Deana Hippie

New York • Toronto • London • Auckland • Sydney
Mexico City • New Delhi • Hong Kong • Buenos Aires

Teaching *Resources*

Stephens Elementary
5687 Hwy. 237
Burlington, KY 41005

~ To Jane Moore, whose generosity of spirit set me on the path that has led to this book and whose steadfast support has opened up opportunities I would never have known

~ To my thousands of students, who gave meaning and purpose to my life

Acknowledgements

Many, many people have helped and supported me over the years, and I wish to thank them.

~ The Corona High staff, who were my professional family for more than 25 years

~ My Teacher to Teacher colleagues, who inspire me with their professionalism and love of teaching

~ Theresa Hinkle, who made it possible for me to present in Houston

~ Everyone at Scholastic, whose faith in me and support made this book possible, especially Sarah Glasscock, whose comments and suggestions helped me write an immeasurably better book

~ My "barn buddies," who share my passion for horses

~ Linda Austin, my dearest friend, who caught the next transcontinental flight when I needed her

~ The Bemis family, my wonderful neighbors, who are angels watching over me

~ Tom, who throughout our life together always loved and supported me and allowed me to be the person I was meant to be

Scholastic Inc. grants teachers permission to photocopy the reproducible pages from this book for classroom use. No other part of this publication may be reproduced in whole or in part, or stored in a retrieval system, or transmitted in any form or by any means, electronic, mechanical, photocopying, recording, or otherwise, without written permission of the publisher. For information regarding permission, write to Scholastic Inc., 557 Broadway, New York, NY 10012-3999.

Cover design by Brian LaRossa

Interior design by Holly Grundon

Editor: Sarah Glasscock

Copy editor: David Klein

ISBN-10: 0-545-11592-2

ISBN-13: 978-0-545-11592-6

Copyright © 2010 Deana Hippie

All rights reserved.

Printed in the U.S.A.

2 3 4 5 6 7 8 9 10 40 16 15 14 13 12 11

contents

Introduction

It was one of those days when I remembered too late the old adage that begins, "Be careful what you wish for . . . " Looking for a new project, I had volunteered to teach a new intervention class for students who had failed the California High School Exit Exam (CAHSEE), but that day I was truly wishing for a less challenging one. About half of the reading comprehension passages on the CAHSEE were expository, so I had decided I should begin there. I instructed my students to read a short passage silently and then asked them recall and comprehension questions, including questions about the main idea of specific paragraphs. My success rate was nil. Finally, I asked students what they *did* recall, and their answer was "nothing." I knew them well enough by then to know that most were trying and that they were being truthful.

My students were also unable to organize and draft an expository composition, and I wondered if this was related to their inability to comprehend and learn from expository text. Since knowing the structure of expository composition—the movement from a general idea to increasingly more specific ideas—is a prerequisite to being both a proficient reader and a writer of expository text, I began to wonder if teaching students the structure of expository text through note taking would improve their reading comprehension and their expository writing.

During the course of my career, I have learned that when a lesson is not successful there are at least two reasons: (1) students lack a conceptual basis or skill, or (2) I have left out a crucial link in their chain of learning and comprehension. Furthermore, I've discovered that if I omit a link in this chain of instruction and learning, my students just "don't get it." The art of the teaching profession is in finding what those missing concepts and skills are and then developing lessons that help students fill in the gaps.

Not too much later, I was introduced to Robert Marzano's meta-analysis of instructional methodology presented in *Classroom Instruction That Works: Research-based Strategies for Increasing Student Achievement* (Marzano, Pickering, and Pollock, 2001). In the first strategy Marzano presented, the ability to see similarities and differences, I found the key to unlocking the puzzle of my students' inability to work with expository text either as readers or writers. And it was the second strategy, the ability to take good notes and write effective summaries, that helped me realize that I needed to develop my students' abilities to read, comprehend, and learn from expository text. Through experimentation, reflection, and revision, I learned how to scaffold the conceptual knowledge and skill-based strategies contained in Marzano's book.

A Tool for All Teachers

Unless students are taught otherwise, many assume that the strategies they use for reading narrative fiction will suffice for reading informational text. They couldn't be more wrong. Not only are the purposes of the two types of writing different, their organizational patterns are also very different. Until we teach our students the organizational pattern of expository text, they will not be able to learn from its content effectively, nor will they be able to write such text well.

As students make the transition from learning to read to reading to learn, they need our continued support to help them make sense of the expository passages they are expected to comprehend and learn from. It is my hope that the lessons in this book will help teachers—in all grade levels and in all subject areas—provide this support. For if we do not provide students with the skills and strategies to access information, all their time and effort will be fruitless; like the students in my intervention class, they will not be able to recall a single thing they read. In that intervention classroom, I learned that if students do not know how to do something, no matter how hard they try, they will not succeed.

How to Use This Book

Note taking and summary writing are skills. No one is born knowing how to do them, yet too often we think that students will develop these skills independently as they're needed. This is not the case. These skills need to be taught directly to students, and we teachers have to become coaches for note taking and summary writing.

The lessons in this book are scaffolded, but after students understand the concepts in Chapter 1 and can use the skills in Chapter 2, you have the flexibility to jump around. If it's more important for your students to be able to develop their skills in taking lecture notes rather than notes on written material, teaching the listening and note-taking skills in Chapter 4 should take precedence over Chapter 3. The skills for summary writing, discussed in Chapter 7, can be taught simultaneously with Chapters 3–6. If you are confident that your students understand the structure of expository text and the concept of categorization, you can begin teaching summary with Lesson 3 in Chapter 7.

Here is an overview of the structure of this book:

Chapter 1: This chapter presents lessons to help students develop the conceptual basis for expository text. The lessons in this chapter are based on Marzano's most effective strategy—the ability to see similarities and differences. Students learn to establish categories and criteria for sorting. After students understand how to sort and classify, they are introduced to the hierarchy of information in expository text: the general or main idea is followed by specific ideas, which are followed by more and most specific information. Students also learn how to color-code text to help them visualize this expository pattern.

Chapter 2: Students learn to identify key ideas and significant details. Oftentimes, they are overwhelmed by the sheer number of words in a passage and have difficulty isolating the truly important information from the words that provide the structure of sentences. Students also learn a system to categorize information and determine which information is important enough to learn and remember.

Chapter 3: The lessons in this chapter teach students to take notes from written text, condensing large amounts of text into a more useful format for learning. The lessons develop students' confidence in their ability to take effective notes and to understand the value and usefulness of text note taking. Alternatives to traditional linear note taking are provided for students who are nonlinear thinkers and processors.

Chapter 4: These lessons help students develop the listening skills necessary for effective note taking. The lessons and strategies support students who do not have a strong auditory modality, ensuring and building upon successful note taking experiences.

Chapter 5: The suggestions in this chapter help students personalize their notes by adding color through highlighting, circling, and underlining. They further personalize their notes by adding sketches and other graphics, personal connections, and so on. Students also learn to condense their notes for review and how to study and review these notes.

Chapter 6: Students apply what they know about text note taking to marking a passage. When students must read and comprehend expository text independently, they need strategies to help them find and return quickly to the key ideas and significant details.

Chapter 7: These lessons develop students' ability to write effective summaries. Summary writing requires the higher-order thinking skills of analysis, evaluation, and synthesis. The step-by-step process taught in this chapter helps students write a summary statement, outline key ideas and significant details, and draft a summary paragraph. Also included are methods for using the summary process for analysis and interpretation of graphical information, such as charts, graphs, maps, timelines, and illustrations.

The Appendix contains reproducibles of passages, graphic organizers, and word lists to help you teach the strategies in this book

Addressing the Different Learning Modalities

Most of the students in my intervention class had a strong kinesthetic modality; therefore, I needed to develop lessons that met their learning needs. Kinesthetic learners have great difficulty dealing with abstract concepts, so I had to create lessons that made the abstract more concrete. Using different colors to identify the concepts of general-specific-more specific information and to show the organization in expository text proved to be a huge help. Also, kinesthetic learners are trial-and-error learners. They prefer to have new concepts presented to them in a way that allows them to experiment with possibilities until they understand the concept, so I began by having them physically sort objects and identify the criterion that was the basis of their decisions.

The strongest modality of most of my other students was visual. Visual learners are attuned to color, placement of text, and formatting cues. These students, too, benefited from the color-coding of the general-to-more specific organization and were able to grasp quickly the formatting aids in textbooks when I pointed them out and explained their function.

The few auditory learners in my classroom benefited from listening to my "think alouds" as I modeled the cognition necessary to learn and use the skills and strategies I was teaching.

The Gradual Release of Responsibility Model for Direct Teaching

In "The Instruction of Reading Comprehension," Pearson and Gallagher explain the Gradual Release of Responsibility Model for teaching students reading comprehension skills; however, the model can be used for the teaching of any skill (Pearson and Gallagher, 1983). The effectiveness of this instructional model comes from talking through the cognition that is required to perform the skill. If students do not know how to think about a task, they will not be able to perform it—no matter how many times they see it done or how many examples we show or model for them.

I encourage you to think of the Gradual Release of Responsibility Model as recursive—as a spiral rather than a line. We remain in a particular stage for as long as our students need us to be there, and if the need arises, we return to a previous stage for re-teaching or reinforcement. The use of the model helps me be a more effective teacher and helps my students reach mastery of skills more quickly.

Here's an overview of the four stages of the Gradual Release of Responsibility Model:

Stage 1: Modeling/Demonstrating
The teacher models while students watch, listen, and copy the teacher's actions.
The teacher "thinks aloud," modeling the cognition required for the task.
Students copy the model that they have seen and heard the teacher create.

Stage 2: Shared Practice

The teacher acts as scribe so students can focus on cognition.
Students begin to "think aloud."
The teacher prompts and guides when necessary.
Students copy the model they have created.

Stage 3: Guided Practice

Students work in small, teacher-created groups.
The teacher monitors and guides when necessary.
Students create the product collaboratively.

Stage 4: Independent Practice

Students work independently.
The teacher monitors and re-teaches when necessary.

In the lessons in this book, Stages 1 and 2 occur in the Direct Teaching-Modeling section. The decision to move to Stage 2 is based on the abilities and needs of your students. Some classes need to spend more time in Stage 1, while others can make the transition quickly. Stage 3 occurs in the Small Group Practice section, and Stage 4 occurs in the Independent Practice section, but not every lesson has these sections. Because students have mastered the skill by Stage 4, I encourage them to use it with their content learning.

Cloze Reading

Sometimes, I suggest you use Cloze reading during a lesson. This strategy helps students focus while someone else is reading aloud. To use the strategy, you will need to preview the passage and identify single words in a few sentences that students can easily pronounce before you display it or hand it out. You read aloud up to one of those words, stop, and have students say the word aloud. You then continue reading. When I first introduce the strategy, I have to try it several times before all students participate.

The following examples use part of the paragraph on page 78 of the Appendix:

Teacher: "Healthy eating requires making wise choices. Selecting fruits and—"

Teacher pauses.

Students: "—vegetables—"

Teacher "—as snacks is a healthy alternative. A crisp apple has few—"

Teacher pauses.

Students: "—calories—"

Teacher: "—and its crunchiness makes it—"

Teacher pauses.

Students: "—satisfying—"

Teacher: "—to eat."

Display Copies

Many of the lessons call for display copies of passages and/or reproducibles. You can create the display copies with clear transparency film for use on an overhead or display the material onscreen.

Guidelines for Note Taking

T-Charts: In this book, I use a T-chart on folded, lined notebook paper as the format for note taking in addition to the reproducible on page 73. I teach my students to create the T-chart on notebook paper because school budget restraints often require that photocopying be kept to a minimum. I explain to my students that this is a modification of the hot dog, or vertical, fold. Instead of folding the paper in half, we take the left side of the paper with the holes and fold it to the margin line on the right side. On 8½-inch x 11-inch paper, the left column is approximately 3½ inches wide. We create the T-chart by drawing across the top line of the paper, and from that line, we draw a line down the crease. We then write the following at the top of the chart to represent the general topic: T =. As we add specific details in the left-hand column, we sketch in a key, and as we note more specific details in the right-hand column, we use bullets. When we add the most specific information, we precede it with a dash.

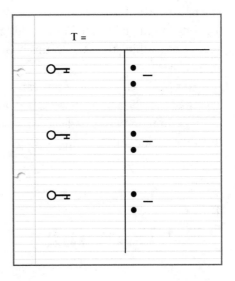

T-chart for Note taking on notebook paper

Skip Lines: After completing the notes for each key, or specific, idea, we skip several lines so the notes are in paragraphs.

The No More Than 4 Rule: To discourage copying entire sentences, I introduce the No More Than 4 Rule: no more than four words per key idea or bulleted more specific idea. Limiting the number of words requires students to look closely at the information and to make decisions about what is significant.

Personalize and Condense: Whenever students take notes, whether from a text or a lecture, they should personalize and eventually condense their notes. See Chapter 5 for suggestions.

Choosing Passages for Instruction in Note Taking

While the structure of expository text generally moves from general ideas to increasingly more specific ones, some written passages do not adhere to this pattern. When choosing passages for teaching note-taking skills, I always ensure that the general-specific-more specific pattern is consistent; for example, in stand-alone paragraphs, the topic is always contained in the first sentence, the second sentence has a specific/key idea, followed by several sentences with more specific and then the most specific information. This specific to more/most specific pattern can be repeated several times within the paragraph. In multiparagraph passages, I ensure that the topic is a stand-alone, a one-sentence paragraph, a boldface topic, or the last sentence in the first paragraph. I want students to focus on learning the skills that I am teaching rather than analyzing the structure of the passage. The passages in the Appendix follow this standard format.

Some Final Thoughts

When teaching the skills of note taking and summary writing, we have one advantage: we can teach *and* practice the skill with content material. All textbooks, including literature books, have expository sections. We can, in effect, accomplish two objectives: (1) to teach or practice the skills of note taking and summary writing and (2) to help students learn the curricular content at the same time. I encourage you to keep this in mind when the enormous demands placed on our instructional time create what seems to be two untenable choices: to attempt to teach the curriculum without teaching the skills to help students master the content or to take time from teaching content to teach the necessary skills. Truthfully, the time you allocate to teaching the skills in this book early in the year will help your students become more efficient learners later.

This book is the result of my learning to teach my students the skills that are essential for their academic success, and my hope is that you will find it valuable for both your own and your students' learning. In retrospect, I understand what a wonderful gift my students gave me on that day they told me that they could recall "nothing."

Bibliography

Marzano, R. J., Pickering, D. J., Pollock, J. E. (2001). *Classroom instruction that works: Research-based strategies for increasing student achievement*. Alexandria, VA. Association for Supervision and Curriculum Development.

Pearson, P. D. & Gallagher, M. C. (1983) "The Instruction of Reading Comprehension," *Contemporary Educational Psychology*, 8, 317–344.

chapter 1

Building Essential Concepts and Skills for Note Taking

We all love a good story: we tell each other the story of our day, stories from our lives, stories that we make up. Stories are read to us as children, and as we become readers ourselves, we continue reading them. They provide entertainment, enrich our lives, and offer insights into what it means to be human. We are taught to read using stories because the suspenseful element of narrative engages our curiosity about what comes next. However, at some point in our education, we are expected to read not only stories but also informational or expository text. Our task then becomes to read to learn rather than to learn to read.

When we introduce our students to expository text, we also need to ensure that they have the conceptual foundation to be able to comprehend what they read. The structure of expository text is very different from that of narrative text. Unless students know this structural pattern of general, specific, and more specific, they will have difficulty making sense of the information they read.

The Purpose of This Chapter

This chapter develops the following conceptual understanding and the skills students need to comprehend expository text:

✶ *Sorting and Classifying:* Unless students can sort and classify, they cannot understand the rhetorical structure of expository text: the movement from the general idea to increasingly more specific ones. Developing the ability to establish criteria for sorting and grouping information is an essential skill for both effective note taking and summary writing. The difficulty is that very often students cannot see beyond the concrete examples to the abstract criterion. Lessons 1–3 lay the foundation for being able to establish criteria. You should expect to work with this concept over time because it requires students to synthesize a new idea from existing information.

✶ *Structure:* Understanding expository structure helps students see the relationship of ideas in what they read and facilitates their comprehension. Having an awareness of this pattern aids students in becoming effective note takers. Lessons 3–6 help them learn the general idea to increasingly more specific ideas pattern found in expository text. They begin by working with words or phrases and move to seeing the pattern in simple paragraphs and then in multiparagraph passages.

Lesson 1: Classifying Specific Ideas Based on a Stated Criterion

Lesson Objective: To learn the concept of using a criterion for sorting objects.

Materials

* Shapes for Sorting reproducible (page 71)

* Animal Pictures for Classifying reproducible (page 72)

* scissors

* four different colors of card stock with magnetic tape backing or colored or clear transparency film (optional)

* pictures with a common theme

Preparation

Copy the Shapes for Sorting reproducible in four different colors: green, yellow, pink, and blue and cut out the shapes. (You can copy it on card stock backed by magnetic tape or colored transparency film or create the shapes on a computer and print them on clear transparency film.) Make a display copy of the Animal Pictures for Classifying reproducible. Gather pictures with a common theme—food stores, sports equipment, and so on—that can be sorted using a number of criteria.

Direct Teaching-Modeling

Display the cutout shapes to students and ask, "What do you see?" After students respond, ask them what they notice about the shapes and note their responses on the board. (Students usually give the following answers: shapes, circles, squares, rectangles, triangles; the shapes are different sizes and colors, and so on.)

Then write the following sentence on the board and have students list as many ways to fill in the blank as they can, for example, size, shape, color: *Some of these objects are the same _____.*

For the next step, write the word *criterion* on the board and its plural, *criteria*, and explain these terms. Here's how I might do this: "When you discover a similar characteristic you can use to group objects or ideas together, you have identified a *criterion* for sorting them. Being able to find a similarity between two objects or ideas helps our brains remember information more easily."

Show the display copy of the Animal Pictures for Classifying reproducible. Tell students that you're going to try to find several criteria to sort the animals and then think aloud: "I notice that some animals swim, some fly, and some walk. However, none of those is a criterion. Swimming, flying, and walking are all *examples* of movement, so the criterion would be 'movement.' I also notice that some animals have fur, others have feathers, and still others have scales. Can someone suggest a criterion for those examples?" (outside coverings of animals)

Students may continue to have difficulty in finding criteria because they focus on the concrete, so keep working with them in establishing criteria for sorting the animals. For example, they can see that some animals live in water, others live in forests, and others live on farms; however, they may have trouble naming the abstract criterion of "habitat" for sorting. You will probably find that you need to move back and forth between Stages 1 and 2. If students cannot suggest a criterion for a list of examples, model your thinking to arrive at one.

Small Group Practice: Give the group pictures from the collection you gathered and ask students to identify three or four possible criteria to sort them.

Independent Practice: Have students draw or collect pictures with a common theme and list possible sorting criteria.

Notes From My Classroom

I work with students on establishing criteria for sorting and grouping information throughout the school year. As my students became more proficient at working with expository text, their ability to establish criteria for sorting and classifying continues to improve.

Lesson 2: Understanding the Hierarchy of General, Specific, and More Specific Ideas

Lesson Objective: To sort objects and create a simple T-chart outline

When I first developed this lesson, I had my students do sorting tasks. For example, I had them sort a variety of items—buttons, beans, ads cut from telephone books, and so on— into piles based on a stated criterion. Later, however, I was unable to transfer their new understanding of sorting into an understanding of the concept of general, specific, more specific information in expository text. We did the lesson again, but this time we created an outline based on their sorting. This laid the foundation for students' being able to understand the structure of expository text. Because we were working with objects, students did not have to grapple with reading and analyzing a passage at the same time they were trying to learn the structure of expository text. Creating an outline at this stage established the format of the graphic organizer we would be using later to take notes. The symbols on the outline and the position of each level of idea are nonverbal cues that my kinesthetic and visual learners could then use to learn the concepts of general-specific-more specific.

Materials

* T-Chart reproducible (page 73)

* shapes from Lesson 1

* variety of objects or pictures (buttons, beans, pictures from magazines, ads from telephone books, clip art, and so on)

Preparation

Create a display copy of the T-Chart reproducible. Students will need lined notebook paper and pencils.

Direct Teaching-Modeling

Show the shapes from Lesson 1 and review several criteria for sorting them into smaller groups. After listing the criteria on the board, review them. For example, you might say the following: "One way we can sort is by using size as the criterion. We can sort the shapes into groups of small, medium, and large. Another criterion we can use is color. We can sort the shapes into groups of green, blue, pink, and yellow."

Then ask students what they know about outlines. (Typical responses usually reveal that students know they're supposed to use outlines when they're writing, and some know that outlines can be used to take notes. The replies show me that most students know when to use outlines but very few know how or why.) Explain that one of the important reasons for making an outline is that it helps us understand how ideas relate to each other. When we have many ideas, we need to sort them into groups that share a common criterion so we can learn the information.

Mix the shapes into one large group and reveal that you're going to sort, or organize, this large group of shapes into smaller groups and then create an outline to show how these smaller groups relate to each other.

Begin modeling how to create an outline by showing the display copy of the T-Chart reproducible. Here's how you might proceed:

"For my outline, I'll use this graphic organizer called a T-chart. My topic is shapes, so I'll write that next to T at the top of the chart. I'm going to use size as my first criterion for sorting the shapes." (I sort the shapes by size: small, medium, large.)

"I've sorted the group of shapes into three smaller groups: small, medium, and large. Do you see the keys in the left-hand column of the T-chart? Next to each key, I'm going to write the name of one of the three groups: small, medium, and large. I can continue to sort each of these three key groups into even smaller groups. For example, I could sort them by color, type of shape, or number of angles. I think I'll sort the small shapes by color." (I sort the small shapes by color: green, yellow, pink, blue.)

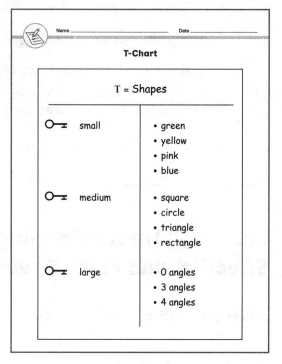

Sample T-chart outline for sorting shapes

"On my outline, I'll list the colors next to the bullets in the right-hand column: green, yellow, pink, and blue. Now I'll sort the group of medium shapes. I could sort this group by color, too, or number of angles or type of shape. I think I'll sort them by type of shape." (I sort the medium group by type of shape: square, circle, triangle, rectangle.)

"I'll write square, circle, triangle, and square beside the bullets in the right-hand column of the outline. Okay, I have one key group left, the group of large shapes. Again, there are several criteria I could use to sort this group: color, number of angles, type of shape. This time, I think I'll sort by number of angles." (I sort the large shapes by number of angles: 0 angle, 3 angles, 4 angles.)

"In the right-hand column, I'll write 0 angles, 3 angles, and 4 angles beside the bullets. Notice what happened each time I sorted a group of shapes: each new group had fewer objects in it. When I did the first sort by size, the original pile was divided into three smaller piles: small, medium, and large. All the objects in each group share a similar characteristic or criterion with all of the other objects: each is small, medium, or large in size. When I sorted the 'small' size group by color, each of the color groups had fewer objects in it than the original group it came from, and each color group only has one color in it."

During the lesson, whenever you feel your students are ready to move to Stage 2 in the Gradual Release of Responsibility Model, ask for their ideas about sorting and categorizing, but scribe for them so they can focus on thinking.

Small Group Practice: Give each student a copy of the T-chart reproducible or demonstrate how to make a T-chart using lined notebook paper (see the model in Guidelines for Note Taking, page 9). Distribute the objects or pictures for each group to sort and outline. Ask students to sort them and create at least three different outlines with at least two key ideas each. (Each student should make a copy of the outlines.) Monitor the groups as they are working and guide and reteach when necessary. Collect the outlines for use in Lesson 3.

Independent Practice: Have students collect their own objects or pictures and then sort and outline them in at least two different ways.

Lesson 3: Understanding the Meaning of General, Specific, and More Specific

Lesson Objective: To learn the meaning of the terms *general*, *specific*, and *more specific*.

K inesthetic learners need concrete experiences with concepts before we introduce them to the vocabulary of the concept. Although my students agreed that they had heard the terms *general*, *specific*, and *more specific* before, they didn't truly understand what the terms meant or how the words related to each other. After seeing the sequence move from a large group to a smaller one to an even smaller one in Lesson 2, they were ready to move into the abstraction of words and terms.

Preparation

Duplicate a copy of the Color-Coding: General → Specific → More/Most Specific Ideas reproducible for each student and make a display copy. Also make a display copy of the T-chart reproducible. Make copies of the General → Specific → More/Most Specific Ideas Sort #1 reproducible and cut apart the sets (make a set for every two students).

Direct Teaching-Modeling

Part 1: Show several outlines created by groups in Lesson 2 and explain that the outlines show how information is presented in most of the textbooks they read and in lectures they hear in school. Then display the shapes outline you created with students in Lesson 2. Label it with the following terms: general (topic); specific (key ideas); and more/most specific (bullets/dashes). Explain that you're going to use a different color to represent each term.

Materials

* Shapes T-chart outlines created in Lesson 2 (display chart and group charts)

* T-Chart reproducible or lined notebook paper (page 73)

* Color-Coding: General → Specific → More/ Most Specific Ideas reproducible (page 74)

* General → Specific → More/Most Specific Ideas Sort #1 and Sort #2 reproducibles (pages 75–76)

* scissors

* three different colors of highlighters or colored pencils for each student

After distributing a copy of the Color-Coding: General → Specific → More/Most Specific Ideas reproducible to each student, talk about the definition of each term and how it relates to what appears on the Shapes T-chart. Then tell students that you're going to use different colors to highlight the terms: "These colors will always represent the same parts of an outline. For example, blue will always be the general idea or topic; green will always be specific/key ideas; and yellow will always be more specific or bulleted ideas and the most specific or ideas with dashes." (These colors are suggestions only. You can choose any colors to represent the three levels of specificity. Consistency is the only requirement.)

Then color code the squares beside each term and the terms. Have students identify the corresponding parts of their own outlines from Lesson 2 and color code them.

Part 2: In the next phase of the lesson, show students a set from the General → Specific → More/Most Specific Ideas Sort #1 reproducible in random order, for example, *two-wheeled vehicle, transportation, motorcycle.* Demonstrate how to arrange the set into the general-specific-more specific pattern, for example: "I have to ask myself which of these is the largest category. Which idea would have the most examples? In this set—two-wheeled vehicle, transportation, motorcycle—transportation is the largest category, or biggest idea, so that is the general idea. What would be the next idea? Well, a motorcycle is an example of a two-wheeled vehicle, so two-wheeled vehicle is the specific/key idea. That leaves motorcycle as the more specific idea. I can check to see if I'm correct by working backward: Are motorcycles two-wheeled vehicles? Yes. Are two-wheeled vehicles used for transportation? Yes. I'm correct."

Copy the words and phrases onto the display T-chart and ask students how to color-code it. Use other sets to repeat the modeling as necessary. Move to Stage 2 when students are ready, scribing their identification of general, specific, and more specific ideas in the sets.

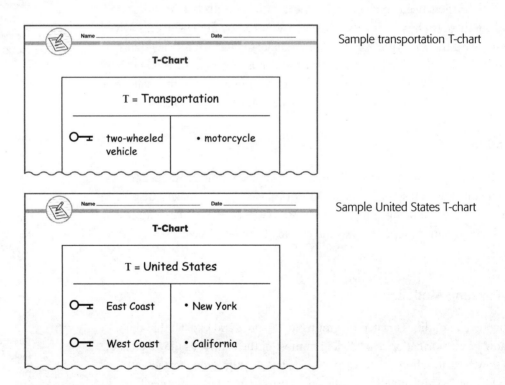

Sample transportation T-chart

Sample United States T-chart

Small Group Practice: Provide students with three sets of ideas from the Sort #1 reproducible, arranged randomly, and have them create and highlight a T-chart for each set. When you feel your students are ready, give them additional specific and more specific ideas from the Sort #2 reproducible, which has groups of five: 1 general, 2 specific/key ideas, and 1 more specific idea for each set.

Independent Practice: Challenge students to create groups of ideas that follow the pattern in the Sort reproducibles and present them to the class as a game in which players compete to see who can sort the ideas quickly and correctly. Remind students to include an answer key.

Lesson 4: Understanding the Rhetorical Structure of Expository Text

Lesson Objective: To correctly reconstruct a five- to seven-sentence paragraph using the concepts of general-specific-more specific ideas.

(*Note:* Depending on the abilities of your students, you may want to work with three-sentence paragraphs in one lesson, five-sentence paragraphs in a second lesson, and seven-sentence paragraphs in a third lesson.)

Once my students understand the concepts in Lesson 3, they are ready to apply that knowledge to understanding the rhetorical structure of expository text. Because many of my students find reading and working with lengthy paragraphs a challenge, I have learned to begin with short passages to build success.

Preparation

Make color-coded (for the general-specific-more specific pattern) sentence strips for the following three-sentence paragraph:

✳ Dogs have been bred for many purposes. One purpose is hunting. Dogs are used to locate game or to retrieve it.

   (You can color code the sentence strips by using different colors of paper, colored sticky dots, or highlighters.)

Make non-coded sentence strips for the following three-sentence paragraph:

✳ Historians have divided the thirteen colonies by geographic region. The regions are the New England, Middle, and Southern colonies. Pennsylvania was a Middle colony.

Also make additional non-coded sentence strips for the expository paragraphs on the Recognizing the Structure of Expository Text on page 77 to use at Stage 2 and Stage 3.

Direct Teaching–Modeling

Part 1: Review the concepts of general, specific, and more specific ideas and the colors you assigned to each in Lesson 3. Then show students the three color-coded sentence strips about dogs and hunting. Read aloud the first sentence and identify and circle the words or phrases that name the general idea; add the second

Materials

✳ Recognizing the Structure of Expository Text reproducible (page 77)

✳ white paper or three different colors of paper

✳ three different colors of sticky dots (optional)

✳ scissors

✳ three different colors of highlighter pens or colored pencils for each student

sentence strip and identify and circle the specific idea; add the third sentence strip and identify and circle the more specific idea. Here's how I would model this process: "The first sentence contains the general idea. You can see that I've color-coded it in blue. The sentence reads, 'Dogs have been bred for many purposes.' 'Dogs' and 'purposes' could both be general ideas, so I'll circle both words. The next sentence is the specific sentence, and I've color-coded it in green. It reads, 'One purpose is hunting.' Now I know that the general idea is 'purposes for which dogs have been bred.' The specific/key idea in the second sentence is 'hunting,' so I'll circle it. The next sentence contains the more specific details, so I've color-coded it in yellow. It reads, 'Dogs are used to locate game or to retrieve it.' The more specific ideas are 'locate game

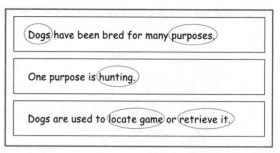

Circled sentence strips, Part 1

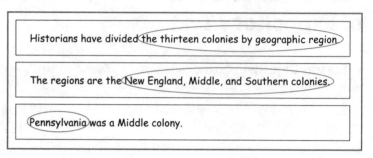

Circled sentence strips, Part 2

or retrieve it,' because they explain what dogs do when hunting.

Repeat this process as many times as needed. In Stage 2, show students color-coded strips for another three-sentence paragraph and ask them to identify the words or phrases that show the general-specific-more specific pattern; circle the words or phrases as students correctly identify them.

Part 2: When students demonstrate an understanding of the identification process, display the sentence strips about the Thirteen Colonies in random order. Model the process of putting them in correct order, circling the ideas and details in the sentences, and using the appropriate color for specificity. Here's how I would model this process of arranging the sentences in order:

"These three sentences aren't color-coded, but because we understand the movement from general to specific to more specific, we can correctly structure them into a paragraph. First, I'll read all three sentences before I make a decision. 'Pennsylvania was a Middle Colony.' 'Historians have divided the thirteen colonies by geographic region.' 'The regions are the New England, Middle, and Southern colonies.' These sentences are definitely not in the correct order. The second sentence contains the general idea: It talks about all thirteen colonies. I'll move it to the beginning. The specific/key idea is in the sentence that names the three regions. I'll move it to the second position. Now the final sentence contains the more specific idea because it identifies one of the colonies in the Middle Colonies."

Then circle the general-specific-more specific ideas in the sentences and color-code them. When you feel your students understand this process, move to Stage 2. Use the sentence stripes you made for the paragraphs on page 77 and have students place the sentences in order. Scribe as they identify the general, specific, and more specific ideas. Color-code the ideas based on students' direction. If students easily grasp the concept, introduce a five-sentence paragraph and guide them through the process of identifying the general idea, the two specific/key ideas, and the appropriate more specific idea.

Small Group Practice: Give each group a set of non-coded sentence strips you created from the Recognizing Expository Structure in Textbook Passages reproducible. Tell students to arrange the sentences in the correct order and have them explain their rationale for the arrangement.

Independent Practice: Give individual students a set of non-coded strips created from content material and have them arrange the sentences in the correct order and explain their rationale for the arrangement.

Notes From My Classroom

Not all paragraphs follow the general-specific-more specific pattern that students discovered in this lesson. However, once students see that there is consistency in expository organization, they are prepared to look more closely at less uniformly organized paragraphs. I have found that the use of color-coding truly helps my students see and understand the structure of expository text and recognize the relationship among general, specific, and more specific information.

Lesson 5: Recognizing the Rhetorical Structure of Expository Text in Paragraphs

Lesson Objective: To identify and color-code the general-specific-more specific pattern in paragraphs.

Up to this point, students have been working with sentences in a paragraph one at a time, but they have begun to see the consistency in the pattern of expository structure. Obviously, they need to transition to working with text in written passages. The transition is usually a smooth one. Because students now have the necessary concepts and skills for recognizing expository structure, they are much less intimidated by longer written passages. I begin with single paragraphs and gradually introduce longer multiparagraph passages as students' confidence increases.

Preparation

Write or collect expository paragraphs of five, six, and eight sentences in length and make copies for students. Create a display copy of the "Types of Literature" passage from the reproducible and duplicate a copy for each student. (*Note:* You can also use another five-sentence paragraph about a topic in your content area. See the other passages on the reproducible for models.)

Materials

* Expository paragraphs with five, six, and eight sentences

* Recognizing the Structure of Expository Text reproducible (page 77)

* three different colors of highlighter pens or tape or colored pencils for each student

Direct Teaching-Modeling

Review the concepts of general, specific, and more specific ideas in expository text and the corresponding colors you've chosen, as well as the process of identifying the words or phrases that can help us determine the level of specificity of an idea. Next, display the "Types of Literature" passage, which is a five-sentence expository paragraph with two specific and two more-specific ideas, and read the paragraph aloud. Then model identifying the hierarchy of ideas in the paragraph. Here's how I would model the process:

"I know the first sentence in an expository paragraph usually contains the general idea. The first sentence in this paragraph is, 'Literature can be divided into two basic types.' 'Literature' and 'types' are the two general ideas. I'm going to circle those words and highlight the sentence in blue, our general idea color. The next sentence should be about a specific type of literature: 'Fiction is one type of literature.' It is; the specific/key example is 'fiction,' so I'll circle it and highlight the sentence in green. Because of the length of the paragraph, I expect that the next sentence will give more information about fiction: 'Fiction is literature that is creative and not based on fact.' It does. The more specific information is 'creative and not based on fact,' so I'll circle that phrase and highlight the sentence in the correct color, yellow."

Continue with the discussion of nonfiction in the rest of the paragraph. Then, if your students are ready, move to Stage 2. Use the "Healthy Eating" paragraph on the reproducible, and have students talk through the process. Circle the words or phrases they suggest and color-code each sentence.

Small Group Practice: Give students several paragraphs of differing lengths and structure and have them read the whole paragraph together, identify and circle the words or phrases that determine generality or specificity, and highlight the sentences in the paragraph.

Independent Practice: Have students complete the steps in the process for identifying the level of generality and specificity of sentences in the "The Best Place to Live" paragraph on the reproducible and highlight it appropriately.

Notes From My Classroom

In a later lesson, you may want to use a six- or seven-sentence paragraph that doesn't have an equal number of more specific ideas. Model the process again, discussing that not every specific idea in a paragraph will have an equal number of more specific ideas. Allow students to talk through the process with another paragraph. If they need additional practice, continue modeling and taking student input until you feel they can work in small groups.

Lesson 6: Recognizing Expository Structure in Textbook Passages

Lesson Objective: To use layout clues to recognize expository structure in textbook passages.

As students progress through the grades, we expect them to acquire more and more information through reading textbooks. For many students, this presents a true challenge for a number of reasons, not the least of which is they do not understand how the ideas are organized. During the time I was experimenting with the previous lessons, I began to question what practical, lasting value these foundational skills that we were building would have once the standardized testing was finished. As a language arts teacher, I had had little experience with teaching expository text, and I began to wonder if there was an application to the content-area textbooks on my campus and discovered that the organization of these books was an extension of the expository composition. Using passages from textbooks, I was able to show students how to apply their new knowledge to their reading of these texts. We also discussed how the layout of the books followed the structure of expository text.

Materials

* Diagram for Recognizing Expository Structure in Textbook Passages (page 79)

* a variety of textbooks

* three different colors of pencils or highlighters for each student

Preparation

Make a display copy of the reproducible and duplicate a copy for each student. Also create a display copy of several sections from the textbooks.

Direct Teaching-Modeling

After reviewing the concepts and skills taught in the previous lessons, explain to students that they can apply their new knowledge and skills when they read their textbooks for information. Then show the display copy of the reproducible. Ask students to look at the passage in the right-hand column and tell you what they notice about its structure and organization. (By this time, they should be familiar with the terminology and can recognize the expository structure.) Fill in the diagram in the left-hand column with the appropriate colors.

Explain that many textbooks use formatting techniques, such as different fonts and type sizes and boldface and italic type, to help readers see the movement from general ideas to more specific information. Point out the difference between reading information in paragraph or essay form and reading in textbooks: In paragraphs and essays, general and specific/key ideas are written as sentences, but in textbooks, they are often just words or phrases that are indicated by formatting techniques.

Then read the passage and analyze its organization. Call on a student to read aloud the title and the three boldface heads aloud. Ask students how the specific/key ideas relate to the title, guiding them to see that the passage is organized by regions. Then ask them to use the title and the section heads to speculate about what information the more specific ideas reveal. After noting students' responses, read the first paragraph using the Cloze methods and confirm their predictions. Have students read the rest of the passage silently to determine if their predictions are still correct.

Stephens Elementary
5687 Hwy. 237
Burlington, KY 41005

To reinforce the connection between the diagram and the passage, tell students to highlight the passage in the appropriate colors. If you feel your students are ready, move to Stage 2. Use one of the textbook sections display copies and have students guide you in drawing and highlighting a diagram of the section.

Small Group Practice: Give students textbooks and have them analyze the organization of a section and draw and highlight a diagram of it.

Independent Practice: Have students analyze the organization of a section they are currently reading, then draw and highlight a diagram of it.

Notes From My Classroom

Although my students had been expected to learn through reading for years, many were unaware of expository structure and how it is used in formatting textbooks. For them, this lesson was a revelation. I suggested that before they began reading, they use the formatting to discover the general and specific/key ideas in the assigned chapter or section by scanning the boldface headings. More than one student told me that for the first time they saw the point of scanning before reading.

Some Final Thoughts

I feel that the lessons in this chapter are among the most important I have developed in my career because they address the root of the problem when students can decode but not comprehend expository text. They also provide the foundation for note taking. Students who truly understand the structure of expository text can easily see the hierarchy of information in what they read. This allows them to find important information more easily and organize it more efficiently.

The use of color-coding to learn about the structure of expository text is invaluable. My students have been told about the general-specific-more specific pattern for years, but when they can actually see it and visualize it, they are finally able to understand it.

Admittedly, the preparation for these lessons is time-consuming. However, once you have collected or written the passages for teaching the lessons, you will always have access to them. Also, if you use card stock for sentence strips, they should last for several years.

My normally disengaged students enjoyed the lessons in this chapter because at the beginning they felt that they were playing games, and later, they participated because they knew how to approach the task. They could, in fact, think "expository text."

chapter 2

Identifying Important Informational Words and Phrases

The following lesson had seemed so simple to me: Circle the important words and phrases in an expository paragraph about theaters in Elizabethan England. As my students and I worked our way through the passage, their difficulty in identifying the words that convey information as opposed to those that provide structure for the sentence became very apparent. I halted the lesson and tried to discover the origin of the problem. I asked students what strategies they had used to decide which words to circle. Their answers amazed me: "I chose the longest word"; "I circled the words I didn't know"; "I didn't think any of them were important, so I just picked one." In the continuing discussion, I discovered that many students are overwhelmed by the number of words in a passage and, consequently, have difficulty in deciding which words or phrases convey important information.

The Purpose of This Chapter

Until students understand that sentences are made up of "meaning" words and "connector" words, they cannot begin to identify the words and phrases that convey important information. Also, students often lack the ability to decide which information is important enough to learn and remember. The lessons in this chapter are designed to help students do the following:

✳ identify important words and phrases in passages

✳ use the 5Ws + H structure to determine whether information is significant

Lesson I: Identifying Informational Words and Phrases

Lesson Objective: To identify the informational words and phrases in a sentence.

Materials

* marker
* scissors
* a variety of expository paragraphs
* three different colors of pencils or highlighters for each student
* content material

When students cannot distinguish between the informational words in a sentence and connector words used to construct it, they cannot be proficient note takers. Students who do not have this skill tend to copy entire sentences from the text or try to write down everything they hear.

Preparation

Make a display copy of the following sentence and cut it into individual words or phrases where the hyphens occur:

* All - living things - are - part of a - food cycle - that - includes - producers, - consumers, - and - decomposers.

Also make display copies of the following two sentences:

* Consumers can be divided into three classifications: herbivores, carnivores, and omnivores.

* Omnivores eat both plants and animals.

Direct Teaching-Modeling

Explain that sentences are made up of two types of words: (1) words that provide information and (2) words that connect these information words to create a complete thought. Display the following words from the first sentence in the Preparation section: *All, are, part of a, that, includes, and.* Model the concept of informational and connecting words. Here's what I might say: "These words are connector words from a sentence. Can anyone tell me what the sentence is about? No? It's impossible because these are words that help us connect information words into a complete sentence. Now I'm going to show you the information words from the sentence."

Display the words *living things, food cycle, producers, consumers, decomposers* and continue to model: "Now we know that the sentence is most likely about living things being part of a food cycle that includes producers, consumers, and decomposers. Let's see if I can combine the connector words and information words into a complete sentence." Compose the complete sentence and show it to students.

Tell students that when they take notes from a lecture or from their reading, they need to make decisions about which words will be most helpful in learning and remembering information. Remind students that complete sentences are never used in note taking, so they have to know how to separate information words from connector words. Emphasize the following: *Taking notes helps us study, learn, and remember information, so we always want to use only those words and phrases that provide information.*

Then display the second sentence from the Preparation section and continue to model the process of identifying information words: "Which words are the information words in this sentence? I'm going to circle (or highlight) the words *Consumers*, *herbivores*, *carnivores*, and *omnivores*. I'm not going to circle *divided*, *three*, or *classifications* because the list of three words—*herbivores*, *carnivores*, *omnivores*—implies the division into classifications. When we

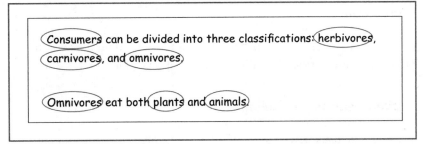

Consumers can be divided into three classifications: herbivores, carnivores, and omnivores.

Omnivores eat both plants and animals.

Informational words and phrases circled in Sentences 2 and 3

take notes, we are constantly making decisions about what to write down. Again, we want to write only the words and phrases that are most important for us to remember."

Display the third sentence from the Preparation section and continue to model. If you feel your students need additional modeling, continue to work at the sentence level; however, if you feel they can now distinguish the informational words, move to Stage 2 and introduce a short paragraph. Read it aloud using Cloze reading and then work with one sentence at a time. Ask students to identify the informational words in each sentence and circle or highlight their responses.

Small Group Practice: Have students work together to identify the informational words and phrases in sentences and paragraphs by highlighting, underlining, or circling them. Use content materials with this activity. If students are working with passages in their textbooks, they should list the informational words in each sentence in a chart like the one on page 80.

Lesson 2: Using the 5Ws + H to Classify Information

Lesson Objective: To introduce the 5Ws + H structure to help students classify information.

Acquiring the skill of identifying informational words and phrases helped my students focus on the purpose of expository reading—to acquire information. I discovered, however, that just being able to access the information didn't mean students understood why it was important. The words and phrases were a hodgepodge that had no true significance for them. Recalling the impact of sorting and classifying, I then designed lessons that would provide students with categories for sorting information, beginning with the basic parts of a newspaper lead: the 5Ws + H. This not only gives students a framework for classifying information but also provides an easy mnemonic when they are trying to identify important words in sentences and making decisions about which words and phrases will be of most importance when they are taking notes.

Materials

* collection of newspaper leads

Preparation

Collect examples of interesting newspaper leads. Be certain they are "hard" news stories rather than human-interest stories. Make display copies of several leads.

Direct Teaching-Modeling

Tell students that a news story—whether print, such as newspapers or magazines, or oral, such as television or radio—begins with a lead. A lead is a one-to-three-sentence summary of the story that follows.

Display a lead and ask students to identify the information words in the sentence, for example: "Yesterday, Roberta Carter, principal of Myersville School, announced the winners of the school's creative writing contest." Explain that a lead always includes who and what happened. Ask students to identify the who and what happened in the lead; in the example: *Roberta Carter* (who) *announced* (what happened). Circle or highlight the words.

Continue by saying that a lead usually reveals where and when and, depending on the news story, how, and/or why. Then identify the purpose of each of the other informational words and phrases in the lead (in the example: *Myersville School*—where, *Yesterday*—when, *winners of the school's creative writing contest*—why the announcement was made.)

Point out that a lead can be thought of as a "five Ws plus an H" sentence: Who, What happened, When, Where, Why, and How statements. Explain to students that using the five Ws + H as criteria will help them identify and sort important information as they read expository text. However, emphasize that not every sentence in an expository passage in an article or a textbook will contain all the parts of the 5Ws + H structure. Read additional expository sentences and have students identify the Ws and the H found in each sentence.

Small Group Practice: Ask students to work together to identify the 5Ws and the H in additional text. This is an opportunity to have them practice using sentences from content that they are currently studying. Students can circle the words if they are using a handout; however, if they are using textbooks, they should assign each sentence a number and list the corresponding words beside each number. (See the chart on page 80.)

Independent Practice: Students can practice the skills learned in this lesson as they read in content areas.

Notes From My Classroom

Students can practice using the 5Ws + H classification structure as they read in the content areas. For example, after reading a short section in their science or social studies book, they can write a sentence about what they've just read that includes as many parts of the 5Ws + H as possible. Using this technique helps students remember important information and write detailed sentences.

Lesson 3: Classifying Information From Expository Text

Lesson Objective: To identify and classify informational words in expository paragraphs.

This lesson begins to transition students from identifying informational words and phrases to writing them down, which paves the way for more traditional note taking. Because students are working with a chart, there is less of a tendency to copy complete sentences.

Preparation

Make a display copy and student copies of the graphic organizer. *Note:* Instead of duplicating it, you can show students how to use a burrito fold to create a three-column chart out of notebook or plain paper. Have them copy the format and headings on the Identifying and Classifying Informational Words and Phrases chart.

Direct Teaching-Modeling

After reviewing the 5Ws + H classification structure, display the Identifying and Classifying Informational Words and Phrases chart. Explain that you're going to use the 5Ws + H structure to identify informational words and phrases in a passage and sort them in a chart. Show the passage and ask a student to read the title aloud. Write it at the top of the chart.

Read aloud the first sentence in the Northeastern tribes paragraph and then think aloud, identifying who and what happened: *tribes lived.* Before recording this under Who/What on the chart, explain that you want to use as few words as possible in the chart but still be able to understand them when you study it later.

Move to the When/Where column, think aloud about whether the first sentence contains any of this information, and note down the following: *Northeast forests.* Explain that it's important to include *Northeast* in the chart because that tells which region you're reading about.

Then ask yourself whether the first sentence contains any information about Why and/or How. Since there is none, leave that column blank. Emphasize that there will be gaps in the chart.

Repeat this process with the second sentence in the Northeastern paragraph. Depending on your students, either continue modeling your thinking with the rest of the paragraph, or move to Stage 2 in the Gradual Release of Responsibility Model. In Stage 2, have a student read the third sentence aloud. Ask the class to identify any 5Ws + H information in that sentence. (If they are confused about leaving the Who/What and When/Where spaces blank, explain that *they* has already been identified, as has the place.) Have students suggest how you should record the information in the chart. (Sometimes students will suggest eliminating prepositions from the phrases. I do ask them to use prepositions at this time but tell them that as they become more proficient at taking notes, I will allow them to make decisions about how few words they can use to communicate meaning.) If the lesson goes well, ask students to work with a partner and complete the chart for the last sentence.

Materials

* Identifying and Classifying Informational Words and Phrases reproducible (page 80)

* "Regional Differences in Traditional Native Homes" passage (page 78)

* plain or notebook paper (optional)

Notes From My Classroom

When my students are capable of independence, I suggest that using the chart is an efficient way to sort and note large amounts of information. Some students find the chart so useful that they ask to use it as an alternative to more traditional notes.

Small Group Practice:

Have students work together to identify important information in the two remaining paragraphs in the passage and record them in charts. You can also give students paragraphs from content-area textbooks. This allows them to practice the skill at the same time they're learning or reviewing the curriculum.

Sample Identifying and Classifying Informational Words and Phrases chart

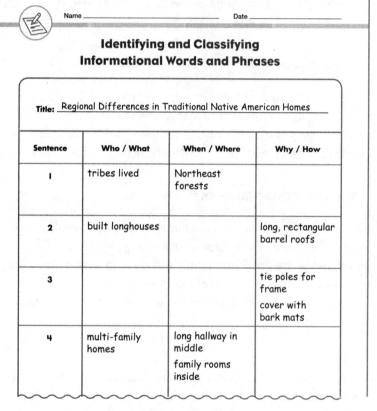

Name _____   Date _____

**Identifying and Classifying
Informational Words and Phrases**

Title: Regional Differences in Traditional Native American Homes

Sentence	Who / What	When / Where	Why / How
1	tribes lived	Northeast forests	
2	built longhouses		long, rectangular barrel roofs
3			tie poles for frame cover with bark mats
4	multi-family homes	long hallway in middle family rooms inside	

Some Final Thoughts

The skills taught in this chapter not only help students identify significant information in expository text but also begin to lay the foundation for note taking. Students learn that not every word is equally important and that if they can identify those that are, they can then begin to organize the information in a way that helps them to learn and remember it more easily. They also begin to realize that note taking is not about copying information, it's about making decisions about what is significant and using the fewest possible words to convey that meaning.

chapter 3

Developing Note-Taking Skills for Written Information

The sheer amount of printed information that students are expected to read and learn each day can be overwhelming. This chapter provides lessons to help students condense large amounts of information into a more manageable and useful format. Traditionally, we have taught students to take notes in a very formal, linear fashion; however, I have discovered that very few of my students are strictly linear thinkers. They need easier options and other formats that support their individual thinking styles and learning modalities.

To be truly efficient as text notetakers, students must understand how expository text is structured—the movement from general ideas to increasingly more specific ideas—so be certain that they understand the concepts and skills presented in Chapters 1 and 2.

The Purpose of This Chapter

The lessons in this chapter reinforce and develop the following skills that students need to take notes on written material:

✴ understand the format and use of the T-chart graphic organizer for taking effective notes

✴ understand the thinking process required for note taking

✴ apply their knowledge of the structure of expository text to take notes

✴ understand how the information in textbooks is formatted and presented

✴ use the formatting of textbooks to take notes while reading

Lesson I: Understanding the T-Chart Format for Note Taking

Lesson Objective: To reinforce the use of the T-chart format for note taking.

Materials

* "The Three Branches of the United States Government" passage (page 81)

* Jigsaw Notes reproducible (page 82)

* scissors

* an envelope for each pair or triad

* colored dots (optional)

* blue painter's tape

With so many strongly kinesthetic learners in my intervention classes, I constantly develop ways to introduce new skills and concepts through the use of manipulatives. While I develop the manipulatives with the needs of those learners in mind, I have discovered that all my students enjoy using them because the lesson looks like a game in contrast to usual instructional methods. Their increased engagement in lessons, and resulting learning, has proven the value of manipulatives for all learners.

Jigsaw Puzzle Note taking is an excellent strategy for introducing the skill of note taking from written information. Students have notes on "puzzle pieces" and the original passage. They use the original passage to arrange the notes in the correct place and in the correct order on a desktop T-chart. The first time I did this lesson, my students asked if they could work together rather than individually. I'm glad I acceded to their wishes because their collaboration resulted in more students "getting it" the first time than I had expected.

Preparation

Make a copy of the passage and the reproducible for each pair or triad. Cut apart the strips in each jigsaw note sheet and place them in an envelope. *Note:* The specific and more/most specific ideas on the jigsaw note sheet are in the correct location and order. You can color-code the strips by adding colored dots if you feel students need additional support in recognizing the structure of expository text. Make a T-chart for each pair or triad with blue painter's tape on a student desk.

Direct Teaching-Modeling

Review the structure of expository text—general, specific, more/most specific ideas. If you're using color-coding, remind students of the color for each level of specificity. After grouping students in pairs or triads, tell them that they are going to use the T-chart on the desk to take notes on an expository passage. Explain that taking the notes will be similar to putting a jigsaw puzzle together. The passage is like the completed picture on the cover of the puzzle box; the jigsaw notes are the puzzle pieces. Their task is to arrange the jigsaw notes in the correct place and in the correct order on their desktop T-chart. If groups have "solved" the puzzle, the order of their notes will match the order of the ideas in the original passage.

Ask a student to read The Three Branches of the United States Government passage aloud. Then have students find the strip in their envelope that reads "T = Branches of the United States Government" and place it above the crossbar of their desktop T-chart.

Reread the first paragraph of the passage together using the Cloze method. Ask students to identify the specific/key idea of the first paragraph (*executive*), locate that strip, and place it in the left-hand column of the T-chart.

Then have students identify the bulleted more specific details, locate those strips, and arrange them in the right-hand column *in the same order as they appear in the passage*:

✳ Direct students to reread the first sentence and identify other important information in it (• *president, vice president*), locate the corresponding strip, and place it in the right-hand column of the T-chart.

✳ Look at the next sentence and identify additional important information (• *proposes new laws, budget*) and add it to the right-hand column under the previous strip.

✳ Have groups finish the first paragraph and stop. Work with students to check that they've correctly identified and arranged the remaining more specific notes for the first paragraph.

Explain that the notes should be formatted in paragraphs just like the text because this allows us to study and review the information in a more efficient fashion. Reread the second paragraph, but before adding notes to the charts, tell students to skip at least two inches below the last bulleted idea in the right-hand column before placing their notes for the second paragraph. Remind students that their notes, like the passage, should always have paragraphs.

Next, have students identify, find, and place the second specific/key idea (*legislative*) and the first more-specific idea (• *Congress*). Encourage students to look at the passage and the strips in their envelopes and tell which two strips come next (- *House of Representatives* and - *Senate*). Point out the dashes and explain that these are examples of most specific information; remind students that we indent most-specific notes and use dashes to identify them.

If you feel your students understand the format of the T-chart and the importance of keeping the ideas in the same order as in the original passage, release the responsibility to them of creating jigsaw notes for the rest of the passage. *Note:* Since this lesson reinforces and extends the use of the T-chart, I don't think extra practice is necessary. However, if you feel your students would benefit from additional practice, you can create jigsaw puzzle pieces for a textbook passage.

Notes From My Classroom

My students truly enjoy this lesson, and, after completing it, they often ask to take notes on strips rather than on a full sheet of paper. I think they find the individual strips far less intimidating than facing a blank T-chart. While we cannot do this every time—and I need to push students out of their comfort zone—I do allow them to occasionally take notes on strips of paper and lay them out on their desks.

For those notes that I want students to keep for learning content, we pick up the strips, beginning at the bottom of the right-hand column of the T-chart and placing each strip on top of the previous one. Each group of more specific strips is covered with its specific/key idea, and the topic or general idea appears on top. We then staple the stack to create a flipbook of notes. Students enjoy using these flipbooks for review because they are tactile and the specific ideas give them clues about the more specific information.

A variation of this strategy is to distribute large note strips to individual students and have them create "Human Notes" by arranging their chairs or sitting on the floor.

Lesson 2: Taking T-Chart Text Notes

Lesson Objective: To take T-chart notes on an expository passage.

Materials

* "Environmental Adaptations of the Desert Tortoise" passage (page 83)

* T-chart reproducible (page 73) or lined notebook paper

The more we work on taking effective notes, the better my students' reading comprehension becomes. When students take notes on what they read, they are actively engaged with the text, making decisions about what information is important, and deciding how to express it in their notes. Also, they work with the passage as a whole rather than looking for isolated bits of information to answer questions, so they see how the various ideas relate to each other. Finally, taking notes helps students present the ideas in a manner that helps them learn, review, and retain the information. Once my students understand the format for taking notes, I teach them the thinking process for it. This lesson models how to make decisions about what is important and how to word the notes as concisely as possible so they'll be useful to study and review later.

Preparation

Create a display copy of the T-chart reproducible and make a copy of the passage for each student and for yourself.

Direct Teaching-Modeling

After having students create a T-chart on lined notebook paper (see page 9), distribute the passage and explain that they'll be taking notes on the chart. Stress that students can reduce long passages into a much smaller, more useful package that will help them learn, review, and remember information.

Then read the title of the passage and write it as the topic of your T-chart. Pause to let students do the same. Using the Cloze reading strategy, read the first paragraph of the passage aloud with students. Ask them to listen to your thinking with their pens or pencils down. After you've finished writing a note, students can copy it onto their T-charts. Give the following guidelines for taking notes:

* Remember the No More Than 4 rule.

* Write each more specific and most specific note on its own line.

* Leave at least one blank line under the T-chart crossbar to make notes easier to read.

* Skip two lines between notes for each paragraph.

Remind students that they can usually find the key idea of a paragraph in the first sentence. To model finding the key idea, think aloud, for example, "From reading the first sentence in the paragraph, I know the specific/key idea for this paragraph is *climate extremes* because it's one adaptation the desert tortoise has made. I don't have to write *adaptation* because it's in the title." (Write the key idea in the left-hand column of the T-chart but leave some space underneath the crossbar.) "I want to use as few words as possible. I need both these words, though, because *climate* can mean too many things, but *extremes* narrows the focus to what I need to remember."

Read aloud the next sentence and continue to think aloud: "The information I need to remember is what the extremes of climate are: *140°F* and *below freezing* are the essential information in this sentence. They give more specific information about extremes of climate." (Write these notes in the right-hand column preceded by a bullet.) Do the same for the third sentence: "*builds subterranean burrows* is important. It gives more specific information about climate extremes. I'll just write down *subterranean burrows* because I'm sure I can remember that the tortoises have to build burrows. I think I also need to remember that *it spends 95% of its life in them*. That statistic is most-specific information about the burrows, so I'm going to indent the line under *subterranean burrows* and use a dash to introduce the idea, *95% of life*."

Read the remaining sentence aloud, modeling your thinking as you decide which information is significant enough to remember, in this case *protects from heat* and *protects while dormant* (most specific ideas). Explain that you can use just those words because you've already made notes about the winter and summer temperatures.

Repeat the process for the remaining paragraphs. If your students are ready to move to Stage 2, ask them to identify the specific/key ideas and important more/most specific details and scribe their responses.

See Chapter 5 for ideas to help students personalize and condense their notes. That chapter also provides suggestions for teaching students how to use their notes for study and review.

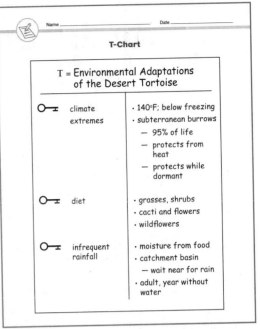

T-Chart Notes for Environmental Adaptation of the Desert Tortoise passage

Small Group Practice: When you're confident that students understand the note taking process, allow them to work together to take notes. Emphasize that everyone must participate and work on the entire passage, not take a paragraph each, and that each student must create his or her own copy of the notes.

Independent Practice: When students demonstrate both confidence and competency in note taking, encourage them to work independently on textbook passages.

Notes From My Classroom

I continue to monitor my students' work, and when necessary, take them through the stages of the Gradual Release Model again. I regularly model taking notes on one or two paragraphs, asking for student input on the next paragraph and then having them work together to complete the passage. Also, I note when students revert to taking too many notes and need to be reminded of the No More Than 4 rule through reteaching and modeling.

The opportunities for students to practice text note taking are many. At first, they can take notes on specific short passages in their textbooks, particularly those that discuss information essential to mastering content standards. As their competence increases, you can increase the length of the passages.

Additional Strategies
for Guided and Independent Note-Taking Practice

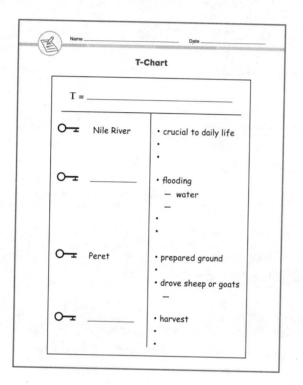

Paragraph	Number of Bulleted More Specific Ideas
#1	(2)
#2	(4)
#3	(3)
#4	(5)

Framed Note Taking

When you provide part of the notes, students have a framework for finding and noting additional information. I create a partial outline with blanks for some of the key ideas and more and most specific information.

Bulleted Note Taking

Students sometimes take too many or too few notes on the right side of the T-chart. Providing the number of bullets needed for each paragraph of text helps them locate the appropriate amount of information. I list the paragraph numbers on the board with the correct number of more specific ideas next to them.

Flash Card Notes

Students can also take notes on 3-inch x 5-inch note cards and keep them on a large ring to use as flash cards for studying. The topic should appear on a separate card. The specific/key ideas are written on one side and the more/most specific information on the reverse side.

Lesson 3: Analyzing the Format of Textbook Passages

Lesson Objective: To analyze the format of textbook passages and understand its purpose.

The time we spend teaching students to take text notes is invaluable. We want them to be able to use these skills to make sense of the enormous amount of print information that they are expected to read and remember. Teaching students to use the format of their textbooks as a structure for taking text notes helps them become more effective note takers. When they understand how to use the bold or italicized headings in their textbooks to organize their notes, the task becomes much more manageable.

Materials

* textbook

* T-chart reproducible (page 73) or lined notebook paper

* three different colors of highlighters

Preparation

Choose a section of a textbook with a format that uses different fonts, type sizes, and/or boldface or italic type to indicate the movement from general to more specific information.

Direct Teaching-Modeling

After reviewing the structure of expository text—the movement from the general idea to specific/key ideas to more/most specific ideas—and the corresponding colors you've previously used, have students open their textbooks to the section you've chosen. Tell them to scan the pages, looking at the different sizes and styles of print and then ask what they notice. As you generate a list of responses, ask what they think their purpose is. If necessary, explain the following:

* Many expository passages and textbooks are formatted to help readers identify important information.

* Formatting includes the use of different fonts, type sizes, boldface and italicized type, bulleted lists, and different colored print.

* Knowledge of what each formatting technique signals helps us to make more sense of the information.

* Usually the type size of boldface or italicized headings is an indication of the movement from the general idea to specific/key ideas and, at times, to more specific ideas; as the information becomes more specific, the type size decreases.

* Bulleted lists are often easier to read than paragraphs and call attention to a list of information that is related; when a bulleted list appears in a textbook, the information in it is often a preview or review of the passage.

* Some textbooks use boldface, italics, and/or different colored print to call attention to important concepts or new vocabulary.

Then read aloud and list the bold headings in the textbook passage. (Depending on your class, have students read the entire passage silently or read it aloud using the Cloze method.) Ask students what pattern they see in the boldface headings and the information beneath each heading, guiding them to see that the largest print is the most general idea, and as the size of the print decreases, the ideas become more specific. Finally, work with students to color-code the headings.

Small Group Practice: Have pairs or small groups look through a chapter or section in the textbook and, on a separate sheet of paper, list the boldface headings and boldface or italicized type in the paragraphs in the order they appear. Ask them to highlight each of the headings in its appropriate color.

Lesson 4: Using the Format of a Textbook to Take Effective Notes

Lesson Objective: To use the format of a textbook passage to take notes.

Materials

* textbook used in Lesson 3

* T-chart reproducible (page 73) or lined notebook paper

Once students understand the purpose of the formatting of their textbooks, you can show them how to apply that knowledge to note taking. However, depending on the grade level, some textbooks may provide more specific information over several paragraphs. To prevent confusion, always analyze the textbook section prior to introducing its structure to students.

Direct Teaching-Modeling

Review the purpose of formatting in textbooks, emphasizing that it shows the movement from the general idea of the section to specific/key ideas to more and most specific ideas. Discuss how the use of formatting can help us take notes more effectively while we are reading the passage.

* Each major topic has its own set of notes. The largest heading is recorded as the topic on the T-chart.

* The first level of subheadings for a section becomes the specific/key ideas on the left-hand side of the T-chart.

* Smaller subheadings under the first level become the bulleted, more specific notes in the right-hand side. Most specific information is listed beneath the bullet, indented, and preceded by a dash.

Then have students use the T-chart reproducible or create a T-chart on lined paper. Read the textbook section using the Cloze method. As students follow your lead, model how to scan the first paragraph in the passage to find and record the ideas in the T-chart. Think out loud to remind students that we take notes in paragraphs and have to skip lines between them, so we cannot list the specific/key ideas in advance.

Continue with the second paragraph. Again, point out that you skip two lines between the notes for each paragraph. When students understand the process, have them to move to Stage 2 and work with you to complete the notes. Scribe their contributions on the T-chart.

Small Group Practice: Have students work together to set up T-chart notes for a textbook section, complete the notes, and share them with another group.

Note Taking
for Nonlinear Thinkers

I find that in spite of direct teaching and ongoing practice, some students still struggle with the semilinear format of T-chart note taking. They need to see information as a totality rather than sequentially. The following nonlinear note taking formats appear at the right: Bubble Cluster, Column Notes, and Idea Tree. I do not teach class lessons on their use; however, I do show these formats to students after I have taught T-chart notes and students have had some practice with the T-chart. I display copies of the nonlinear note taking formats and tell students that these are other possibilities for note taking, and they are free to choose one or even to create their own. I assure them that they are free to adapt the strategy to meet their needs as long as they show me that they are taking notes and learning the information.

The Picture Web shown at the right is a combination of webbing, listing, and drawing that many of my students find to be an effective note-taking strategy. The topic is written in the center and the specific/key ideas are webbed from it. Students then add a combination of written and picture notes. Some teachers have their students create a class Picture Web on chart paper at the end of a chapter or chapter section and post it in the room. The Picture Web provides an easily accessible, ongoing review of previously learned material. These webs are also useful for showing students themes that run through the curriculum.

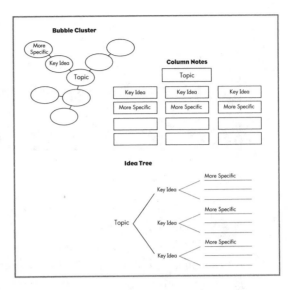

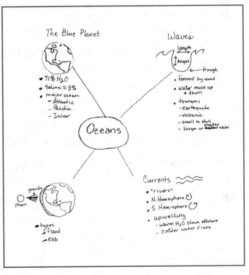

Some Final Thoughts

At some point in my career, I heard the advice that as we begin to teach skills, we need to go slow at the beginning to go fast later. When I realized that my students did not truly realize the power of taking text notes, I had a decision to make: Should I spend the time teaching them to take notes, or should I push ahead with the content that I was expected to cover? I recalled the "go slow to go fast" rule and realized that the time I spent teaching students to take text notes early on would allow them to learn content later with more efficiency and greater mastery—and it did.

chapter 4

Developing Note-Taking Skills for Oral Information

When my students had become proficient text note takers, I felt certain that they could transfer their skills to taking notes during a lecture. However, I quickly realized that this wasn't the case. Taking lecture notes is a very complex task. The note taker has to listen, make almost instantaneous decisions about the relative importance of the information, and note it down. Because I had assessed my students' learning modalities, I knew that very few of them had a strong auditory modality, making learning from lectures a challenge. I also realized that I needed to develop lessons that addressed each requirement for taking effective lecture notes. Through trial and error and a great deal of reflection and adjustment, I have developed a scaffolded series of skills that builds students' confidence and increases their feelings of competence as note takers.

The first tier of lessons works on students' ability to listen to a lecture and remember information. To ease some of the frustration of being asked to do so many things at the same time, students do not take notes at this tier. Once students have confidence in their ability to listen for information, they move to the second tier, where they recognize key ideas and significant details as they hear them. In the final tier, students first listen and take notes on only the key ideas as they hear them. As their proficiency increases, they begin to take notes on the more specific information as they listen. At the beginning of each new tier, I use short passages of no more than three to five paragraphs, depending on the skill level of my students.

Finally, remember to regulate the speed at which you read or lecture. When you move to a new tier in the lesson scaffold, slow your speech and pause at the end of each paragraph or after each section of key idea and more specific information. These pauses give students a chance to catch up on their notes, reducing their frustration with a demanding task.

The Purpose of This Chapter

The lessons in this chapter help students develop the following skills they need to take notes while listening:

* take notes using pictures, reviewing the pictures, and adding written notes

* listen to and remember information and write it down during a pause

* use framed notes to make notes while listening

* identify and note key ideas while listening

* take notes while listening, including title, key ideas, and more specific ideas

Lesson 1: Taking Picture Notes

Lesson Objectives: To practice using pictures to take notes.

When I began teaching students to take picture notes and then add written notes, they became more engaged in their lessons. We use picture notes for both expository and narrative passages, and I gradually increase the length of the passages and the amount of time I read or lecture. Students tell me that the pictures trigger additional ideas that they can write down and that pair-share helps them acquire the information that they missed.

Materials

* 2 expository passages (each three to four paragraphs long)*

* Picture Notes reproducible (page 84)

  * This lesson uses "Regional Differences in Traditional Native Homes" (page 78).

Preparation

Make a display copy and a copy of the Picture Notes reproducible for each pair of students. On the day before teaching this lesson, ask a student to be the reader of the first passage and suggest that he or she practice reading it aloud. On the day of the lesson, write any unfamiliar or difficult-to-spell words on the board.

Direct Teaching-Modeling

Display the Picture Notes reproducible and point out the line at the top for writing the title of the passage, the spaces in the left-hand column for sketching notes, and the spaces in the right-hand column for adding words and phrases. Then tell students that, with the help of the student-reader, you're going to model how to listen to a passage and take picture notes. Here is how you might model taking picture notes:

"Audrey, will you please read the title of the passage and then stop?"

(Write the title on the display copy of the Picture Notes reproducible when the student pauses.)

"Audrey, will you please read the first paragraph and then stop? I'm going to put down my pen while I listen. I'm not going to take any notes while Audrey reads."

(When the student stops reading, begin to sketch what you remember about the first paragraph in the left-hand column of the Picture Notes reproducible.)

"Now I'm sketching what I remember about the first paragraph. I'm going to draw a tree and a longhouse. This picture will help me remember that the Northeastern Indians lived in the forests in longhouses."

Repeat the process for the rest of the passage, listening and then drawing a sketch for each paragraph. When the student-reader finishes the final paragraph and you've completed your picture notes, explain that you're going to review the pictures and sketch in other details or add words to the sketches. Think aloud as you do so, for example:

"When I look at my sketch, I remember that this house was in the Northeastern forests. So I'll write *Northeastern forests* next to the first bullet in the right-hand column. I also remember that the houses were called *longhouses*, so I'll write that next to the second bullet. Several families lived in each longhouse, so I'll write *several families* next to the last bullet."

Then ask students to supply other details, written or pictures, to add to the right-hand column.

Small Group Practice: Have pairs alternate between making suggestions for sketches and drawing them. Distribute a copy of the Picture Notes reproducible to each pair. Read each paragraph of an expository passage, pausing for about 45 seconds to allow time for suggestions and sketching. (You can adjust the time for your students, but the idea behind the skill is to draw quickly.) When you've finished reading the passage, ask pairs to review their sketches and jot down additional details that they remember. Finally, have each pair join another to discuss and review their notes. Students should add any information they learn from the other partners to their own notes.

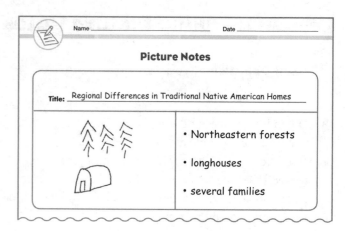

Sample Picture Notes sheet

Independent Practice: Ask students to take picture notes as they listen to lectures, watch presentations or videos, and so on. After they have added written details to their picture notes, ask them to participate in a pair-share or whole-class share-out.

Lesson 2: Taking Two-Pass Notes

Lesson Objective: To practice the two-pass note-taking strategy.

Materials

✳ two expository passages (each three to five paragraphs long)*

✳ Two-Pass Notes reproducible (page 85)

✳ markers (two different colors)

✳ colored pens or pencils for students (two different colors)

    * This lesson uses "Regional Differences in Traditional Native Homes" (page 78).

Two-pass note taking provides a bridge from taking notes in pictures to taking notes in words. It gives students another chance—a second pass— at hearing information through the repetition of the reading or lecture or the sharing of information. I use three techniques for the second pass:

(1) At the beginning, when I am teaching the two-pass note taking process and want to emphasize the importance of careful listening, I reread the passage or redo the lecture while students jot down any information they missed the first time.

(2) As students become more attentive, I ask them to use pair-share. Each partner adds any information he or she missed the first time.

(3) When the information is essential for content mastery, I use whole-class share-out, moving through the notes one by one and making certain that each student has recorded all the essential information in the chart.

Preparation

On the day before teaching this lesson, ask a student to be the reader of the first passage and suggest that he or she practice reading it aloud. Make a display copy of the Two-Pass Note Taking reproducible and a copy for each student. Write any unfamiliar or difficult-to-spell words on the board.

Direct Teaching-Modeling

To begin the lesson, display the Two-Pass Note Taking reproducible and give a copy of the reproducible to each student. Point out where to write the title of the passage. Tell students that they would write the topic here when they're listening to a lecture. Then explain that the numbers in the left-hand column indicate the number of paragraphs in a passage, or the number of times the reader will stop. During the pauses, you'll write down key words and phrases that you remember in the left-hand column next to the appropriate number. Then model how to listen and take two-pass notes. Here is how your modeling might look:

"Samir, will you please read the title of the passage and then stop?"

(When the student stops, hold up one of the markers.)

"For my first-pass notes, I'm going to use a red marker. I'll start by writing the title at the top."

(Have students copy your work. When they have done so, I ask the reader to continue.)

"Samir, will you please read the first paragraph and then stop? I'm going to put down my marker while I listen. I'm not going to take any notes while Samir reads."

(When the student stops reading, think aloud as you write your responses in the left-hand column next to the number 1.)

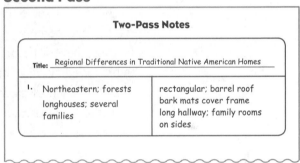

First Pass

Two-Pass Notes

Title: Regional Differences in Traditional Native American Homes

1. Northeastern; forests
   longhouses; several
   families

Second Pass

Two-Pass Notes

Title: Regional Differences in Traditional Native American Homes

1. Northeastern; forests
   longhouses; several
   families

   rectangular; barrel roof
   bark mats cover frame
   long hallway; family rooms
   on sides

Sample Two-Pass Notes sheet

"I remember that Native Americans in the Northeast lived in forests in longhouses. Several families lived in them. I'm only going to write down key words and phrases: *Northeastern; forests* and *longhouses; several families*. Remember the No More Than 4 rule—no more than four words for each thought and no complete sentences. This is the first paragraph, so I'll write those words next to the number 1."

Since this is the first pass, deliberately leave out some information. The second pass will give you the opportunity to add information you missed the first time.

Then pause for students to copy your notes. Proceed to the second paragraph. Put down your marker and ask the student-reader to read the second paragraph; at the end of that paragraph, call on three students to share one idea that each of them remembers. Write their ideas in the left-hand column next to the number 2. Again, deliberately omit some information, even when students volunteer it; explain that you'll use that information later. Pause to let students copy your notes.

After the student-reader finishes the third paragraph, ask students to work in pairs to write down what they remember next to the number 3. (If you're working with a longer passage, continue having students work together to note down the information they remember next to the appropriate number.)

Tell the student-reader to read the first paragraph again. Hold up the second colored marker and reveal that you're going to use it for your second-pass notes. Write down any information you missed during the first reading in the right-hand column. Have students use the second colored pen or pencil to copy your additional notes. After listening to the second paragraph, call on students to provide the missing information and then write it in the right-hand column. Pause while they copy the information. When the student-reader has read the third paragraph, have students work in pairs to fill in any missing information.

Students easily master this strategy. The security of knowing that they will have a second opportunity to hear the information makes them willing to participate. I believe that your students, like mine, will be ready for independent practice very quickly and that you will find many opportunities to use this strategy. However, if you feel your students need additional practice, they can take notes in pairs and triads with each student creating a copy of the group notes.

Notes From My Classroom

If your students can only process one or two ideas at the beginning, adjust your think-aloud to reflect that. As students become more proficient, add more information. I have discovered that students can remember numerical facts and statistics more easily than abstract ideas, so I use passages with dates, speeds, height, weight, and so on when beginning to teach the skill and gradually reduce the amount of numerical information.

As students become more confident about their ability to listen and remember information, they will begin to feel more comfortable noting the information as they listen because they know that they will have a second opportunity to hear what they missed the first time. If students ask whether they can try to take notes while I'm reading or lecturing instead of waiting for me to pause, I always let them. However, I never require all students to make the attempt at this point.

Using the two colors of pens holds students accountable for participating throughout the lesson. I can look around the room and see who has been working for the entire lesson because the amount of information in each color indicates the student's effort. The two colors also provide an ongoing assessment of each student's developing proficiency because the amount of information in the first color indicates his or her ability to listen and take notes.

Two-pass note taking is particularly effective when you introduce new content to students. A brief note taking lesson on the new information not only provides an advance organizer for students but also allows them to practice their new skills. A K-W-L chart is a wonderful advance organizer, but when students don't have any knowledge of a topic, these charts lose their value. Two-pass note taking can provide some basic knowledge about new content that allows students to begin a K-W-L chart.

An alternative to rereading the second pass is to have students do pair-share or small-group share or whole-class share-out. I use the whole-class share-out when I want to ensure that all students have access to the information. Throughout the scaffolding of lessons in this chapter, I continue to give students a second opportunity to acquire the information because it lessens their frustration about note taking.

Lesson 3: Taking Framed-Bulleted Notes

Lesson Objective: To take notes while listening to a passage.

W hen my students have developed confidence in their ability to remember oral information, I begin to transition them to the next tier of the scaffold: the ability to listen and take notes at the same time. To accomplish this, I support students by framing the notes. I provide the key ideas from the reading and then have them listen and note *some* of the more specific ideas as they hear them.

Because by this point my students have developed confidence in their ability to take notes during lectures and reading, I'm usually able to model the process using just two of the four paragraphs in a passage and then move to independent practice.

Preparation

On the day before teaching this lesson, ask a student to be the reader of the passage and suggest that he or she practice reading it aloud. Choose an expository passage with one key idea per paragraph. Create a display copy of the T-chart. Duplicate a copy for each student or have students use lined paper for the T-chart instead (see page 9 for directions).

Direct Teaching-Modeling

Explain that the objective of the lesson is to begin to move toward taking notes while listening instead of waiting for a pause, but reassure students that they will not be responsible for writing down all the information they hear. They are taking the first steps and are not expected to immediately master this skill.

On the T-chart, list the title of the passage, the specific/key ideas for students to copy in the left-hand column, and the number of bullets for each key idea in the right-hand column. (I ask for about half of the more specific ideas in the passage. For example, if there are four more-specific ideas about a key idea, I give students a target of two.)

Then pass out the copies of the T-chart reproducible, or have students create one on lined paper. Ask them to copy the specific/key ideas from your T-chart and add the appropriate number of bullets in the right-hand column beside each key idea. Remind students to skip two lines after the last bullet beside each key idea so their notes are in paragraphs. Explain that your goal is to write one specific idea next to each bullet, but that the passage contains more specific ideas than there are bullets—however, they are only responsible for the number of bullets on the T-chart.

As the student-reader reads the passage, have students watch you take notes. Ask the reader to read more slowly than usual. When you hear the first key idea, point to the first key idea in your chart. Then, as you hear the more specific details, note them next to the bullets. (In your modeling, try to get one bulleted idea from the first part of the paragraph and one from the middle or end of the paragraph.) When you hear the second key idea, point to that key, write the key idea, and finish taking the notes in the right-hand column.

Materials

* expository passages (three to four paragraphs long)

* T-Chart reproducible or lined notebook paper (page 73)

* markers (two different colors)

* colored pens or pencils for students (two colors each)

At the end of the second paragraph, emphasize that you were able to take notes on about half of the specific details. This should be students' goal as well, and assure them that they will have an opportunity to note all the information in a share-out later.

Take over the reading and return to the beginning of the passage. Read slowly and emphasize when you move to the next key idea. When you finish your first read-through, have students change to a different color of pen and add additional notes as you read the passage again. At the end of your second read-through, do a pair-share or whole-class share-out to support those students who may not have been able to complete the notes.

In later sessions, gradually increase the number of bullets in the chart and continue to read slowly, building students' ability and confidence in hearing and noting more specific ideas. Practice often. Continue to list the specific/key ideas on the board or on screen, provide a target number of bullets, and remind students to skip two lines after the last bullet for each key idea. You don't have to practice with long passages. Using two-to-three-paragraph passages for review or preview of content information two or three times a week develops and reinforces the skill and provides repeated access to important content material.

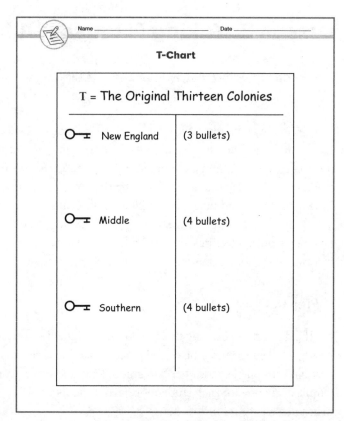

Sample Framed Bulleted Notes T-Chart (Display Copy)

Lesson 4: Using Transition Words to Identify Key Ideas

Lesson Objective: To use simple transitions to identify key ideas when taking notes on oral information.

To be truly proficient note takers, students must be able to identify key ideas as they hear them. When first teaching this skill, I use explicit transitions, such as *first, also, another, finally* at the beginning of each new specific/key idea. If students already know transition words, this lesson should be a quick review of transitions and their purpose of introducing a new key idea.

Preparation

Make copies of the Expository Transitions Bookmark for each student and cut them apart. Also make a copy of the Two-Pass Note taking reproducible for each student or have students create their own on notebook paper. Write any unfamiliar or difficult-to-spell words on the board.

Direct Teaching-Modeling

Introduce or review the purpose of transitions—to signal a new idea. I find that using the analogy of comparing transitions to road signs helps students understand their purpose. Just like road signs that read "Stop Ahead" or "Curves Ahead" alert drivers to a change in road conditions, transitions alert readers to a change in ideas. These changes include introducing or adding another specific or key idea, changing the direction of the discussion, signaling a comparison or conclusion, and so on.

After distributing the Expository Transition Bookmarks, review them with students, explaining that when they hear or see one of the transitions in a passage, they should be prepared for a new specific idea.

Then discuss the changes in the use of the two-pass note-taking format. Instead of listening for information in the passage and writing it down after a pause, students will listen for the transition that indicates a new key idea. When they hear the transition word or phrase, they will immediately write it next to the correct number on the Two-Pass Note taking sheet. In this lesson, they will not write anything in the right-hand column.

Read the passage just a little more slowly than you normally would. After the first paragraph, pause to ensure that students have correctly identified the transition word.

When students can easily recognize the transition when they hear it, move to the second step. This time students listen for the transition words or phrases in the passage and use them as a clue that a specific/key idea is coming up. When they hear the specific/key idea, they write it next to the appropriate paragraph number and the transition, separating the transition and key idea with a comma. Again, read the passage just a little more slowly than normal and stop after the first and second paragraphs to ensure that students have written down the correct key idea. At the end of the passage, have students compare their answers with a partner's.

Materials

* expository passage with clear transitions (three to four paragraphs long)

* Expository Transition Bookmark reproducible (page 86)

* Two-Pass Notes reproducible (page 85)

* scissors

First Pass

Two-Pass Notes

Title: _Three Kinds of Rocks_____

1. one	
2. another	
3. third	

Second Pass

Two-Pass Notes

Title: _Three Kinds of Rocks_____

1. one, igneous	
2. another, sedimentary	
3. third, metamorphic	

Sample Two-Pass Notes, With Transitions

Small Group Practice: If your students need additional practice, divide them into pairs. Read aloud passages with explicit transitions for key ideas and have them work together to identify and write down the transitions. As an alternative, you can have them give a thumbs-up or raise their hands when they hear the transition word.

Lesson 5: Taking Complete Notes While Listening

Lesson Objective: To take complete notes—including general topic, key ideas, and more specific ideas—while listening.

Materials

* expository paragraph with clear transitions* (three to five paragraphs long)

* T-chart reproducible or lined notebook paper (page 73)

* markers (two colors)

* colored pens and pencils for students (two colors each)

* This lesson uses "Hummingbirds: Mother Nature's Flying Jewels" on page 87.

When students have mastered the skills in the previous lessons in this chapter, I expect them to take notes independently. However, I continue to support them in ways that ensure their ultimate success. Because students are now responsible for taking notes on the complete passage, I return to shorter passages with fewer key ideas and specific details and give the number of specific/key ideas and the more specific ideas they should expect to find. Knowing the number of more specific ideas I expect them to write down helps reduce students' anxiety and focus their attention. I also continue to reassure students that they will still have a second chance to pick up any information they missed through pair-share or whole-class share-out.

Preparation

On the day before teaching this lesson, ask a student to be the reader of the passage and suggest that he or she practice reading it aloud. On the day of the lesson, create a display copy of the T-chart or draw it on the board. Include the number of key ideas and of bulleted more specific ideas in each paragraph. Make a copy of the T-chart reproducible for each student or have them create their own on lined notebook paper (see page 9). Write unfamiliar and difficult-to-spell words on the board.

Direct Teaching-Modeling

Ask the student-reader to read the passage at a normal speed and stop reading when you raise your hand. This pause will give you the time to think aloud. At the first pause, model your note-taking process. Here's how your modeling might begin:

Ask the student-reader to begin with the title. (After hearing the title, repeat it and write it next to the T =.) Tell the student-reader to read the passage.

(At the end of the first sentence, raise your hand.)

"The first sentence tells about how colorful hummingbirds are. I'll write *color* in the left-hand column as the first key idea."

(At the end of the first paragraph, raise your hand.)

"The rest of the paragraph describes the colors of males and females. In the right-hand column, I'll write *males: brilliantly colored* beside the first bullet. Under that, I'll write *females: dull colors*. I remember the No More Than 4 rule, so I don't want to write too many words. I know, too, that I can come back and add more details."

Then ask students to copy your notes. Before moving to the second paragraph, remind them to skip two lines between each key idea so that notes are in paragraphs just like the passage.

If your students need additional modeling of the thinking necessary for taking notes, remain in Stage 1 of the Gradual Release of Responsibility Model. Have the student-reader continue with the second paragraph and model listening to and noting down the specific/key ideas and the more specific information.

If your students are ready to move to Stage 2, ask the student-reader to read the second paragraph. Tell students to raise their hands when they hear the specific/key idea. Call on a volunteer and write his or her response in the left-hand column after skipping two lines. Continue with the rest of the paragraph, scribing students' responses about the more specific ideas. At the end of the second paragraph, pause while students copy the notes.

Small Group Practice: Have pairs take notes as you read or lecture. One of the partners should raise a hand for you to stop and the other writes down the information after the two confer.

Independent Practice: Use a two- to three-paragraph passage and challenge students to listen and take notes at the same time. Continue to provide the number of the specific/key ideas and more specific ideas. Assure students that they will have a second pass at the information if they need it, but they must attempt to take notes while you're speaking. Slow your speech and pause briefly at the end of each paragraph. Over time, speak more normally and shorten the pauses at the end of paragraphs.

Notes From My Classroom

I provide students with many opportunities to practice their note taking—and it can be practiced in many different ways: guest readers, video clips, morning announcements, brief lectures to preview or review content material, and so on.

Some Final Thoughts

Taking notes while listening is a complex skill. Students must listen to a flow of words and make immediate decisions about separating specific/key ideas from more specific details and about the relative importance of the information they are hearing—and write it all down.

Teaching students to be effective note takers also teaches them to be effective listeners. The process takes time initially; however, as students become more confident in their skill, they become more engaged in class, and when you use content material to practice, you'll make up the time later.

chapter 5

Personalizing, Studying, Reviewing, and Condensing Notes

Personalizing notes helps students create a context for new information by creating ownership of their notes. They choose the words and phrases in their notes that have the most meaning for them, and they create nonlinguistic clues for information. Teaching strategies for personalizing notes also provides students with additional opportunities to learn the information because they have to review their notes to carry out the tasks. Personalizing notes involves the techniques of adding color by highlighting, underlining, boxing, or circling essential words or phrases in the notes and adding pictures or other graphics to represent the information. Some students use the three colors representing the general-specific-more specific pattern; however, using just one or two colors is also acceptable.

Since notes are effective only if used, we need to teach students how to use their notes for studying and reviewing and provide a timetable that promotes the acquisition and retention of information.

Finally, as students master the information, they need fewer word or picture cues to remember what they have learned. We then teach them how to condense their notes for ongoing review of what they have learned.

The Purpose of This Chapter

The lessons in this chapter help students develop the following skills that they need to personalize, study, review, and condense notes:

✴ emphasize essential words in notes by adding color

✴ add graphic representations to notes to more easily recall information

✴ use notes for effective study and review

✴ condense notes for easier review of information

Lesson 1: Emphasizing Essential Words in Notes

Lesson Objective: To select and emphasize the most important words or phrases in notes.

This lesson shows students how to make decisions about which words in their notes will be most helpful in learning, reviewing, and recalling information and to emphasize the words or phrases through the addition of color. As students decide which words to emphasize, they begin to change their notes from just words on a page into an effective, individualized learning tool.

Materials

✳ Student or teacher notes (Save for Lessons 2–4)

✳ Highlighters, markers, or colored pencils

Preparation

Make a display copy of either your notes from a previous lesson or a student's.
Ask students to choose notes they made in a previous lesson or in another subject area.

Direct Teaching-Modeling

Explain that personalizing notes helps us learn and remember information more easily. We want to make the most important words and phrases in our notes stand out because they help our brains "unlock" and remember the rest of the information. Ask students to watch and listen as you make decisions about which words and phrases will be most helpful when you're studying and reviewing your notes later.

Then display the notes you're going to use to model this process. If the general topic or title contains more than one word, ask: "Which one or two words are the most essential? I can do one of the following to emphasize these words—underline, highlight, or circle them. Today I'm going to highlight them with a marker. So I'll highlight the words *Hounds* and *Hunt* in the title. *Dogs* is a synonym for *hounds*, so I don't need to highlight it. The other words, *of* and *the*, don't reveal any important information."

Work through the notes from general to specific to more specific information and continue to discuss which words or phrases are essential to remembering the information.

Ask students what other ways they can think of to make the important words stand out in their notes and assure them that any of their suggestions are acceptable because everyone is personalizing his or her own notes.

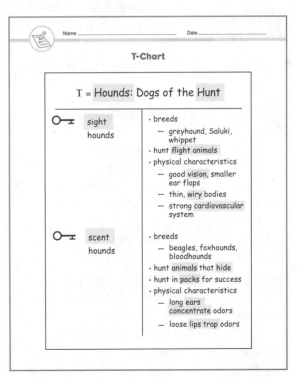

Sample for Lesson 1

At the beginning, be very direct about how many words and phrases students can highlight—usually one or two words in the topic or title, one word in each specific idea, and depending on the length of the more/most specific ideas, four to six words per paragraph of notes. Without these limits, students tend to highlight almost everything rather than making decisions about which information is essential. The highlighting, boxing, circling, and so on, in color, emphasizes words and phrases in notes and is valuable in and of itself because the markings draw the eye to key words and phrases. Equally important, it also requires students to review their notes in order to make effective choices. Later, as students review their notes, they'll use these words to help them recall the other information in the notes.

Independent Practice: Have students review their own notes to decide which words and phrases are essential to remember and choose a method to emphasize them.

Lesson 2: Adding Graphic Representations to Notes

Lesson Objective: To add pictures or other graphics to represent information in notes.

Materials

* Display copy of teacher notes from Lesson 1

* Student notes from Lesson 1

* highlighters, markers, or colored pencils

Two or three days after students add color to their notes is the optimum time for them to review their notes again. During this second review, I ask students to add sketches to their notes. The transfer of verbal information into a graphic representation provides a key to unlock the information stored in long-term memory. When adding sketches to their notes, students choose pictures that connect to previous learning or experience, strengthening their ability to remember new ideas.

Direct Teaching-Modeling

Remind students that the purpose of personalizing notes is to make them more useful for study and review. Then explain that adding pictures or other graphics to notes can make them even more personal; pictures and other graphic representations are like keys that can help us unlock information stored in our brains.

Ask students to watch and listen as you review your notes and make decisions about what you can sketch on the notes to make them even more personal and helpful. Display your notes from Lesson 1. Think aloud as you decide what kind of picture will help you remember the information in the first paragraph. For example, you might say:

"I could sketch an eye to represent sight, but that might not be enough to remind me that the topic is hunting dogs. Another possibility is sketching a dog's head with an arrow pointing to its eye (pause to think). I don't think that's the best idea because not all dogs are sight hounds. I'm going to review my notes I have about sight hounds. I see that sight hounds are similar to greyhounds, so I'll draw a greyhound with large eyes and a running deer. These two sketches will help me remember not only that these hounds locate prey by sight but also the breeds, flight animals, and physical characteristics."

Ask students if they can think of any other possibilities and emphasize that there is no best or right way to create a picture for notes because the only person for whom the picture has to make sense is the note taker.

Sketch your picture in the left-hand column underneath the specific or key idea. If necessary, continue with the rest of the paragraphs; however, if you're confident that your students understand what to do, release the responsibility to them.

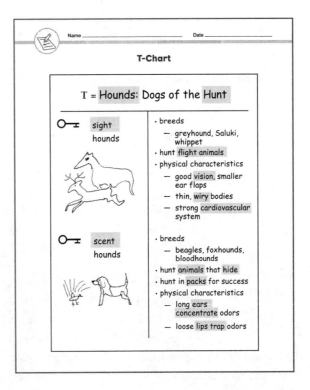

Sample for Lesson 2

Notes From My Classroom

I find that most students master this strategy quite easily. Therefore, I can release responsibility to them after modeling at Stage 1. When a student is having trouble finding an idea for a picture, I make a suggestion and ask other students what they drew for that part of their notes. This often helps the student move forward. However, I always emphasize that the best pictures to include are those they create themselves. The pictures students choose themselves create a personal connection to the information and draw on their own background knowledge or previous learning, so they are more likely to remember the information.

Pictures are not the only possibility. Some of my students have used the names of people, books, or movies. My more linear thinkers have used mathematical representations and charts and graphs. I also emphasize that if the original picture or graphic isn't proving useful in unlocking other information, students can replace it with another one.

I often ask students to explain why they chose a certain picture or other representation, and their answers always give me an insight into their thinking processes. During the conversations, I begin to understand which students are global thinkers and which are more linear. Not only do I begin to understand my individual students better, I am also reminded that my teaching must accommodate both thinking styles.

Lesson 3: Using Notes for Study and Review

Lesson Objective: To learn a process for studying and reviewing notes.

Materials

* Display copy of teacher notes from Lessons 1–2

* Student notes from Lessons 1–2

* Blank sheets of paper for teacher and students

Teaching students a timetable for study and review will help them use their notes more effectively. Notes should be reviewed and studied for the first time within 24 hours of being taken. During the first review, students should emphasize essential information through highlighting or using colored pens or pencils to underline, circle and so on. The second review and study should happen within two or three days, and at this time, students should add pictures or other clues to their notes. From that point on, study and review should take place on a regular basis; weekly is the optimum interval.

No matter how well students take notes, they are not effective unless students know how to use them to learn and review information; therefore, we need to directly teach and rehearse with students how to use their notes to both learn and review information. Setting aside time each week for students to review their notes will promote their retention of information and provide multiple opportunities for them to learn and then review information.

Direct Teaching-Modeling

Tell students that just reading and rereading notes does not help our brains organize information. To do this, we need a system that follows the general-specific-more specific pattern. Then show the display copy of your personalized notes and cover the right-hand column with a blank sheet of paper. Read aloud the first specific idea in the left-hand column and think aloud, for example, "When I read this section of my notes and look at my sketch, what do I remember about this idea?" Recite some of the information you remember, but omit about half of it. Then uncover the right-hand column and read aloud the more specific information in it, emphasizing which information you remembered and what you still need to learn. Finally, cover the right-hand column again and recite the information you remember for the second time.

At this point, have students practice the strategy with one paragraph of their own notes. Ask for their feedback about the process: "What did you notice about your use of the strategy? Why do you think studying and reviewing notes in sections is more effective than simply reading through them?"

Small Group Practice: Have students work together to study their notes, taking turns reciting information aloud and quizzing each other by asking what each knows about the specific ideas. Later, ask them to show the partner only his or her picture for each specific idea so the partner can recite the specific/key idea and the more specific ideas.

Independent Practice: When students are able to study and review their notes independently, allow them to choose to work with a partner or on their own.

Lesson 4: Condensing Notes

Lesson Objective: To condense notes.

Direct Teaching-Modeling

Begin by explaining that after using notes to learn and study information, you still need them for ongoing review so you can retain the information. Condensing notes onto index cards helps us review them on a regular basis. Point out that as students have personalized their notes, they've made decisions about what is important in the notes: (1) They've emphasized essential information through highlighting, underlining, and so on, and (2) they've represented a great many words in a single drawing or graphic.

Tell students that in a sense, they've been continuously condensing their notes. A final step in this process is to create note cards using their graphics and a few key words or phrases.

After displaying a copy of your personalized notes, explain that you'll use the first note card for the topic or title. Write the title or topic on an index card. After completing the title card, tell students that you'll use one note card for each paragraph of your notes. On the front of a new index card, draw the picture associated with the first paragraph of your notes; on the back, write the specific/key idea and then three to five important words or phrases. As you do so, emphasize that you want to choose the words that will unlock the most information.

Allow time for students to work through the process with two or three paragraphs of notes.

Materials

* Display copy of teacher notes from Lessons 1–3

* Student notes from Lesson 1–3

* One 3-inch x 5-inch or 4-inch x 6-inch index card for each paragraph of notes

* colored markers, pencils, or pens

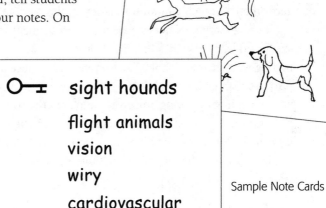

sight hounds

flight animals

vision

wiry

cardiovascular

Sample Note Cards

Some Final Thoughts

As my students learn to personalize their notes, their ability to use them for effective study and review increases. I think this is primarily because the words they choose to emphasize and the sketches or connections come from their own experiences—they now have ownership of them. Also, being taught how to use notes for study and review and being shown how to condense notes onto small cards changes their perception of the purpose of note taking. They begin to see the taking of notes as the first step in creating a valuable tool for learning, rather than just an academic exercise.

chapter 6

Developing Text-Marking Strategies

We want our students to be able to use all types of note-taking strategies in their learning process. However, we also need to recognize that in high-stakes testing situations, knowing how to make in-text notations is critical because of the large amount of reading required. Teaching students text-marking strategies accomplishes two objectives. First, students are more focused on what they are reading because they are making decisions about what to mark. Second, they are emphasizing words and phrases that will allow them to quickly find information in the passage to answer test questions.

In-text marking strategies are not a replacement for text notes. Very few students can use them to study and learn new information. At least once a year, a student asks why they can't just take notes by highlighting their textbooks like they've seen college students do. I explain that marking text has a different purpose than taking text notes. When we mark the text while reading, we focus our attention on what we are reading by asking ourselves which are the truly important words and phrases that will help us find information to answer questions. However, the purpose of text notes is to help us study and review information. To show the difference, I put a marked passage and the resulting text notes side by side. Students see that the text notes are more useful as a study tool because the important information has been isolated and reduced to just a few words.

The Purpose of This Chapter

The lessons in this chapter review or develop the following skills that students need for marking text while reading in order to find information quickly and to answer questions:

✳ identify general, specific, and more specific information through the use of color-coding

✳ identify and mark only essential informational words in a passage while reading

✳ learn alternative strategies for text marking

Lesson 1: Reviewing How to Color-Code a Paragraph

Lesson Objective: To review color-coding a paragraph by identifying general, specific, and more specific information.

The prerequisite skills for this lesson were taught in Chapters 1 and 2, so the amount of time you spend on this lesson will depend on your students' level of mastery.

Preparation

Make a display copy of the paragraph and a copy for each student.

Direct Teaching-Modeling

Tell students that you're going to review some of the skills they have already learned. Then display the paragraph and read it using the Cloze method. Ask student to help you color-code the paragraph to find the topic, specific/key ideas, and more specific ideas.

Usually, I only need to demonstrate one paragraph, because by this time, students have internalized the structure of expository text as general-specific-more specific ideas. However, if your students need additional instruction or practice, provide it by having them work together to practice and review color-coding.

Materials

* expository paragraph with two or three specific/key ideas and more specific information

* highlighters, pens, or colored pencils (three different colors for each student)

Notes From My Classroom

I use highlighters in the teaching process for the text-marking strategy, but I also transition students to using pens or colored pencils and underlining or circling essential words. A highlighter obviously places the emphasis on words or phrases and makes them stand out, but this tool cannot be used on certain tests. When students master the strategy through the use of highlighters, the transition to underlining or circling is easy.

Lesson 2: Identifying and Marking Essential Information

Lesson Objective: To identify and mark only the essential information in a passage.

Materials

✳ Model Paragraphs With Different Purposes reproducible (pages 88–89)

✳ highlighters, pens, or colored pencils

Preparation

Select two or three paragraphs from the reproducible. Make a display copy of each one and a copy for each student.

Direct Teaching-Modeling

Explain that in this lesson you'll be making decisions about which words or phrases to highlight as you read. Review the purpose of in-text marking and how it's done: The purpose is to locate information in a passage efficiently. This is done by eliminating non-essential words or phrases and highlighting as few words as possible to find information when answering questions.

Display the first paragraph, read the title, and think aloud about which words to highlight and to eliminate (this modeling is based on the sample on the next page): "I need to highlight both *Advantages* and *Disadvantages* so I'll remember that both will be discussed in the passage. I'm also going to highlight *Solar Power.*"

After reading aloud the entire paragraph, return to the first sentence and reread it. Ask yourself which words will help you find information when answering questions about the paragraph and then model your answer: "I don't have to highlight *Sun* because I have highlighted *Solar* in the title, and that's a word related to the sun. I don't want to highlight any words that I've already highlighted or any synonyms for those highlighted words. I'll highlight *delivers more energy* and *every two weeks* because that's one of the advantages of solar power. I'll also highlight *found, all,* and *fossil fuels* because they will help me find information to answer questions later. I won't highlight *oil* and *coal* because they're examples of fossil fuels and I've already highlighted that phrase."

Notes From My Classroom

I find that unless I regularly reteach text-marking strategies with a least one or two paragraphs, my students begin highlighting too much information The lure of the "runaway highlighter" is too strong to resist for long.

Reread the second sentence and model your thinking: "I don't have to highlight *advantages* because I already did that in the title. *Inexhaustible* is a definite advantage, and I know what the words means, so I'll highlight that instead of *it cannot be used up.*"

Continue to reread each sentence and model marking the essential information and explaining your decision-making process. When your students are ready, work with them in marking a new paragraph. Ask a student to read aloud the entire paragraph as the others follow along. Then call on individual students to tell you which words and phrases to highlight and to explain their reasons for their choices.

Small Group Practice: Have students practice the strategy as you monitor. Stress the importance of stating the justification for their choices. Ask groups to compare their marked passages and explain why they highlighted the words they did.

Independent Practice: Assign a short passage for homework. The following day, tell students to compare their highlighting with a partner and explain their reasons. Then ask questions based on the passage and have students raise their hands as they locate the information.

The Advantages and Disadvantages of Solar Power

Although the sun delivers more energy to Earth every two weeks than can be found in all of the fossil fuels, such as oil and coal, that exist on our planet, solar power has both advantages and disadvantages. One of the advantages is that solar power is inexhaustible; it cannot be used up. Also, solar power is clean energy. It does not create exhaust or poisonous waste products. One of the disadvantages is that solar energy is not concentrated but is spread thinly across the surface of the Earth. Another drawback is that the power is not constant. Solar power can only reach Earth in the daytime. Also, some areas of the planet do not receive enough solar energy to make it an efficient alternative to fossil fuels.

Sample Marked Passage

Some Final Thoughts

I think in-text marking is the most neglected note-taking skill. Yet, for our students who must read long passages of informational text, particularly in testing situations, it is truly important. This strategy helps students maintain focus while reading and locate information quickly. Because my students have had experiences with deciding which information in a text is important in lecture and text note taking, they are able to master this strategy in a relatively short period of time. However, I do have to continually remind them that in the case of in-text marking, less is definitely more.

Additional Strategies
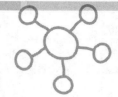
for Guided and Independent In-Text Marking Practice

You can introduce the following strategies when students understand the purpose and process of text-marking. I demonstrate the strategy, but I do not move through all the stages of the Gradual Release of Responsibility Model. I allow my students to adapt the strategies to their needs; however, they must always demonstrate that they understand the purpose of text marking.

Circling and Underlining
Once my students master the concept of in-text marking, I transition them to using pens or pencils in case they are in a situation where highlighters cannot be used. We regularly practice test-taking strategies, and during this time, I limit them to using only a pen or pencil. Students can choose to underline, circle, or box words and phrases. Some students have developed the strategy of circling the key/specific idea and then underlining the essential words in the paragraph.

Highlighter Tape
Highlighter tape, available in various sizes, can be used for in-text marking on non-consumable products, such as textbooks. I put a variety of lengths of highlighter tape on a piece of transparency film and distribute them to students. Students use the lengths of tape to highlight in their textbooks and then replace them on the film for storage.

Number Please
This strategy helps students make careful judgments about what to highlight. I choose a number of words that can be highlighted in a paragraph; students can highlight up to that number. I begin with about 10 words and then gradually reduce the number to four or five. This is easy to assess and grade because the choices students make truly show whether they understand the strategy and whether they have read the whole paragraph before making those choices.

Cut and Paste
Students who thrive on kinesthetic activities will enjoy cutting and pasting. Print a paragraph or two on a colored sheet of paper. Increase the type size and line spacing so that essential words and phrases can be cut out of the paragraph and pasted on another sheet of paper in the approximate position they held in the original paragraph. The colored paper mimics the highlighting, and the resulting "markings" demonstrate the concept of specific/key ideas and significant details.

Developing Codes
Demonstrate to students how margins can also be used for in-text marking. A self-developed symbol code written in the margins can help students locate information quickly; for example, a box can indicate an important person; a circle, an important date; a triangle, a place; a capital C, a cause; and a capital E, an effect. The possibilities are endless. Stick-on notes can be used in nonconsumable materials.

Pictures in the Margin
Visual learners can locate and recall information that is represented in graphics. Adding pictures in the margins not only helps visual learners locate information quickly but also helps them remember the information.

chapter 7

Writing Summaries

After having my students read a lengthy article, I asked them to write a brief summary of it. After sighing, groaning, and rolling their eyes, most of them began to write. However, the results showed that their idea of a summary was to list what they remembered rather than to provide a short, organized recap of the main idea of the article and its specific/key ideas and significant details. My students needed an understanding of the purpose of summary writing and a structured strategy for writing an effective one.

The Purpose of This Chapter

In *Classroom Instruction That Works*, Robert Marzano concludes that the ability to take good notes and to write effective summaries is a powerful strategy for helping students learn, second only to seeing similarities and differences. The skill of summary writing is complex, involving multiple higher-order thinking skills including analysis, synthesis, and categorization. Clearly, students need a structured, sequential strategy for this task and ongoing practice.

Summary writing involves the following three steps:

1. Creating a three-part summary statement that (a) names the passage, (b) states its purpose, and (c) summarizes the specific/key ideas into a main idea, using categorical terms

2. Selecting and outlining the specific/key ideas and choosing the most significant details

3. Writing the summary passage

These three steps are taught in Lessons 6–8. Lessons 1–4 deal with the prerequisite skills for summary writing: the ability to determine the purpose of a passage, to categorize, to group ideas and objects based on a shared criterion, and to identify that criterion. Summary writing is, in essence, a form of note taking. Both entail condensing large amounts of information into key ideas and significant details. However, if summary writing is used after note taking, it reintegrates those key ideas and significant details into a prose format. When students have mastered note taking, summary writing can, in effect, become their note taking strategy. All the lessons in this chapter will help students review or develop the following skills they need to write effective summaries:

✳ determine the purpose of a passage

✳ review categorizing

✳ identify categorical terms for abstract ideas

✳ state the purpose of a passage and categorize its specific/key ideas

✳ understand the requirements of a summary

✳ write a complete summary statement

✳ create a Key Idea Outline

✳ write a summary paragraph

Lesson 1: Determining the Purpose of a Passage

Lesson Objective: To analyze a passage and determine its purpose.

Materials

* Purposes for Expository Writing reproducible (page 90)

* Model Paragraphs With Different Purposes reproducible (pages 88–89)

Whenever students read an expository passage, we should ask them to determine its purpose. Knowing the purpose of a paragraph helps them to understand its organization and to learn the information it contains.

Preparation

Make a display copy of the Purposes of Expository Writing reproducible and a copy for each student. *Note:* You may want to divide this lesson into two or three parts, so students become familiar with two or three specific purposes at a time. Also, make a display copy of one of the paragraphs on the Model Paragraphs With Different Purposes.

Direct Teaching-Modeling

Explain that informational or expository passages are written for a variety of purposes including to list information; to describe people, places, or objects; to show steps in a process; and so on. Then distribute the Purposes for Expository Writing reproducible to students. Review each purpose and its description. If necessary, teach the vocabulary required, for example, *comparison* and *contrast*.

After displaying the model paragraph from the Model Paragraphs With Different Purposes reproducible, read it aloud. Then ask students to listen as you think aloud to decide its purpose and give evidence to support your ideas. For example, you might say, "The paragraph on Athens and Sparta shows the ways in which they were alike, for example, *Both Athens and Sparta were powerful city states.* It also shows how they were different. For example, in Sparta the boys were *trained to be army officers*; while in Athens, the boys were *enrolled in academies* to learn about a variety of subjects. Therefore, the purpose of the passage is to compare and contrast."

The most effective time to directly teach and model how to identify a particular purpose is just prior to having students read a passage with that purpose in their textbooks or other materials. I model my thinking process aloud with a sample passage, citing text evidence for my observations, such as "shows ways they are alike and ways they are different" and drawing a conclusion by stating the purpose. Then, I have students read the passage for that day's content lesson and ask that they use the same process to determine the purpose of the passage.

Whenever students work on reading passages in small groups or independently, they should determine the purpose or purposes of the passage after having read it.

Lesson 2: Reviewing Categorizing

Lesson Objectives: To review the concept of categorizing and identifying a categorical term for concrete objects.

When writing summary statements, writers often need to use categorical terms, such as *characteristics*, *causes*, *effects*, or *ideas* for the specific and more specific information in a passage. This lesson is a review of the concept of categorization students learned in Chapter 1.

Direct Teaching-Modeling

Materials

* Sample Lists for Categorization reproducible (page 91)

Begin the lesson by telling students that you are going to review categorizing. Remind them that a category is a word or phrase that explains the characteristic shared by several objects or ideas, and give an example, such as the following: "The category *transportation* includes cars, trains, airplanes, bicycles, and so on. All of these objects move people or freight from one place to another."

Read aloud the first list on the Sample Lists for Categorization reproducible—without giving away the category: "Preschool, elementary, middle school, high school, college. What characteristic do all the examples have in common? They are all places of learning, so they belong to the category of *schools*."

Repeat with additional lists on the sheet, calling on individual students to identify which characteristic the examples share and to name the category until you feel students recall or have learned the concept.

Small Group Practice: If students seem to need additional reinforcement, provide additional lists from the reproducible and have them work together to categorize the terms. Students can also create lists of related terms and share them with the class, which then identifies the shared characteristic and category.

Lesson 3: Identifying Categorical Terms for Abstract Ideas

Lesson Objective: To identify a categorical term for abstract ideas.

This lesson can be repeated to introduce the categorical words that students need when they learn new content. For example, if a science lesson is about acid rain, introduce the terms *causes* and *effects*. This skill is often the most difficult part of teaching summary writing because students are required to analyze the information in the passage and then synthesize an abstract categorical term or terms. However, through repetition and ongoing rehearsal, my students become familiar with the categorical terms and learn when to use them appropriately.

Materials

* Categorical Terms for Summary Writing Bookmark reproducible (page 92)

* scissors

Preparation

Copy and cut apart the Categorical Terms for Summary Writing Bookmarks reproducible so each student has a bookmark. Create a list of physical characteristics, such as *6 feet tall, 180 pounds, brown hair*, a list of actions, such as *running, jumping, talking*, and lists for other categorical terms appropriate to your curriculum.

Direct Teaching-Modeling

After reviewing the concept of categorization, stating how a group of objects and ideas are alike (see Chapter 1, pages 12–15), show students the list of physical characteristics. Ask them to complete the following statement: *These are all examples of _____.* List students' responses on the board. If no one knows the words *characteristics* and *traits*, introduce the words and explain that these are two categorical terms that are helpful in describing how people or things look.

Next show the list of actions and ask students to complete the above statement. If no one suggests *actions* or *behaviors*, introduce these words. Because the purpose of this lesson is to introduce new categorical terms as students need them, you will not need to move beyond the direct teaching stage because students will use the new terms immediately.

Lesson 4: Stating the Purpose of a Passage and Categorizing the Specific/Key Ideas

Lesson Objective: To write a sentence that states the purpose of a passage and categorizes its details as a main idea.

Materials

* Model Paragraphs With Different Purposes reproducible (pages 88–89)

* Verbs for Summary Writing reproducible (page 93)

A summary statement uses an active verb to identify the purpose of a passage and a global statement that categorizes the specific information in the passage. On the surface, this seems to be an easy task; however, it requires that students use both analysis and synthesis. Because of the complexity, I find that many students need multiple instances of direct teaching-modeling and guided practice, or Stage 2 in the Gradual Release of Responsibility.

To state the purpose of a passage and categorize the details in it, a writer must do the following:

* identify the purpose of the passage

* select a corresponding verb

* categorize the significant details as a main idea

* insert additional words

Preparation

Make a copy of the reproducibles for each student and distribute them.

Direct Teaching-Modeling

Remind students that all expository passages have a purpose and that they have learned how to categorize lists of details. Explain that you are going to write a sentence that states the purpose of a paragraph and categorizes its specific/key ideas. Then use the Cloze method to read "Bats," the first paragraph on the reproducible, aloud. After asking students to identify the purpose of the paragraph, model how to create a sentence that states the purpose and categorizes the details in it. Here's what you might say:

"My goal is to write a sentence that states the purpose of the paragraph and categorizes its specific/key ideas. I know the purpose of the paragraph is to provide information about the topic of bats, so I'm going to look at the Verbs for Summary Writing sheet for verbs that go with this purpose. I could use any of them, but I think I'll use the verb *describes*. Next, I want to be find a categorical term for the significant details in the paragraph. When I read the paragraph, I learned several ways in which bats are helpful to humans. For example, bats pollinate plants and eat insects that damage crops, and scientists are studying them to help people. All of these are things that help people, so a categorical term for the specific/key ideas is *benefits*. Now I can write a sentence that states the specific purpose of the entire paragraph: *The paragraph describes the benefits that bats provide to humans.*"

If necessary, work through several more paragraphs on the reproducible using the same procedure. When you feel your students are ready, move to Stage 2 of the Gradual Release of Responsibility Model. After reading the paragraph together, call on a student to state the purpose of the paragraph, and ask another student to suggest a verb that you can use to state the purpose. Have students tell you what the key ideas are and list them on the board. Then ask students to suggest possible categorical terms to cover the key ideas.

Small Group Practice: Provide students with other paragraphs from the reproducible that have different purposes and ask them to work together to write a sentence that describes the purpose of the paragraph, using verbs for summary writing, categorical terms, and additional words to extend the sentence. Later, have students repeat the process with their textbook reading by asking them to write a sentence that identifies the purpose and categorizes the details in the section.

Independent Practice: When students have had multiple opportunities to practice this skill with guided practice and small group practice, ask them to independently create statements of purpose and categorize details as a main idea after reading in their textbooks.

Lesson 5: Understanding the Requirements of a Summary

> **Lesson Objective:** To state the requirements of an effective summary.

Materials

* "Learning Preferences" and Summary reproducible (page 94)

Effective summary paragraphs have a three-part topic sentence that (1) identifies the passage; (2) uses an active verb to state the purpose of the passage; and (3) provides a global statement about the key ideas in the passage. The rest of the sentences in the summary state the key ideas and most significant details about those ideas. Summaries also use categorical terms for details. For example, if a passage lists several flowers, such as *roses, carnations, petunias,* and *daisies,* the categorical term *common garden flowers* might be used. Summaries usually do not have a conclusion, and the writer of the summary does not comment on the information.

Preparation

Make a display copy of the reproducible and a copy for each student.

Direct Teaching-Modeling

Explain that summaries are useful tools for remembering information and that there are requirements for an effective summary. Tell students that today they'll be looking at an original passage and a summary of it, and they'll identify and label parts of the summary.

Then display "Learning Preferences" and its summary. After reading the passage and the summary aloud, explain that the topic sentence of a summary has three parts: the first part names the title, author, and genre of the passage; the second uses an active verb to state the purpose, and the third gives the key ideas of the passage by categorizing the specific

details. Ask students to underline the summary topic sentence (the first sentence). Show them how to use vertical lines to divide the topic sentence into its three parts and identify each with a letter: N (Names), P (Purpose), M (Main Idea).

> *N*
> The article "Learning Preferences," by Jason Evans
> *P* | *M*
> describes | the characteristics of the three learning
> modalities. (Visual) learners learn by studying (graphics) → *categorical term*
> and watching demonstrations. Text formatting and the
> location of information assist them in learning and
> remembering. (Auditory) learners need to hear and
> discuss information. Oral communication is important
> to them, but organizing writing may be difficult.
> To "hear" as they read, they may move their lips.
> (Kinesthetic) learners are grounded in reality, learning
> by doing and experimenting. Concrete examples of
> abstract ideas help them understand. They need to see
> "big pictures" before they can learn the details.
> *No Conclusion*

Sample Marked "Learning Preferences" Summary Statement

Have students identify the three specific/key ideas in the original passage and then locate and circle them in the summary statement. Explain that only really important more specific information should be included, so they have to make choices about what to include. Ask students to compare the more specific information in the original passage with what is included in the summary and decide whether they agree with the choices and why. (This will give you a chance to explain that summaries are like notes in paragraph form. Not everyone will make the same choices.)

Then explain that one way to summarize information is to use categorical terms for details in a passage. For example, if the original passage used the words *hawks*, *eagles*, and *owls*, you could use the categorical term *birds of prey* or *raptors* in your summary. Ask students to find a place in the summary where a categorical term, in this case *graphics*, is used in place of details. Have them draw a box around the word or phrase and then draw an arrow to the margin and write "categorical term." Finally, tell students that summaries do not usually have a conclusion, and ask them to write "No Conclusion" at the bottom.

Notes From My Classroom

I emphasize that summary writing is not a substitute for note taking, but it is a final step in learning and studying expository text.

Lesson 6: Writing a Complete Summary Statement

Lesson Objective: To write a three-part summary statement

When students have become proficient at writing sentences that identify the purpose of a passage and categorizing its details, they are ready to write a complete summary statement.

This lesson also demonstrates how students can use the notes they have taken to help them write the summary statement.

Preparation

Prior to the lesson, have students take text notes on "Hummingbirds: Mother Nature's Flying Jewels" or a passage of your choice that has at least two key ideas. Make a display copy of your own notes for the passage you have chosen for the lesson. Instead of using the Creating the Summary Statement reproducible, you can use a half sheet of lined paper folded into three vertical columns (a burrito fold).

Direct Teaching-Modeling

Explain that in today's lesson you'll be writing a complete summary statement, a sentence that has the following three parts:

Materials

* "Hummingbirds: Mother Nature's Flying Jewels" passage (page 87)

* Teacher and student notes on "Hummingbirds: Mother Nature's Flying Jewels" from Lesson 5

* Creating the Summary Statement reproducible or lined notebook paper (page 95)

* Verbs for Summary Writing reproducible (page 93)

* Categorical Terms for Summary Writing Bookmarks from Lesson 3

✳ The first part names the title, author, and genre of the passage.

✳ The second part uses an active verb to identify the purpose of the passage.

✳ The third part states the main idea of the passage, using categorical terms.

Point out to students that they have already been practicing how to write the second and third parts of a summary statement.

Display the Creating the Summary Statement reproducible or have students create a burrito fold, draw lines in the folds, and copy the following headings to create a chart: *Name It, Tell the Purpose (Verb),* and *Write the Main Idea.* Point to the first column and say that you'll write the title, author, and genre of the passage there. Because students have had practice in identifying the purposes of passages, ask them to identify the purpose of this passage, and after referring to the Verbs for Summary Writing chart, write the active verb they choose in the second column of the chart.

Then tell students that they're going to look at their notes on the passage to write the last part of the summary statement. Ask them to review their text notes to identify the specific/key ideas. List students' ideas on the board and then have them refer to their Categorical Terms for Summary Writing Bookmark for suggestions of categorical terms that fit the key ideas.

When I teach this skill, I find that I need to repeat Stage 1 and Stage 2 of the Gradual Release of Responsibility Model several times. Its cognitive complexity and the multiple steps need repeated demonstration and guided practice. Consider having students write summary statements daily on anything they read, hear, or see.

Small Group Practice: Have students work together to write summary statements of reading passages, lectures, audiovisual materials, Web sites, and so on.

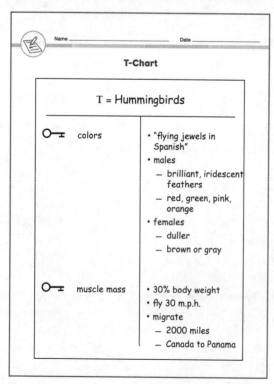

Based on the notes, the summary statement is "Hummingbirds: Mother Nature's Flying Jewels" describes the physical characteristics and behavior of these tiny creatures.

Lesson 7: Creating the Key Idea Outline

Lesson Objective: To create a summary outline of the key ideas and most significant details of a passage.

Preparation

Make a display copy of the Key Idea Outline reproducible and duplicate a copy for each student. Instead of using the reproducible, students can copy your display copy on a half sheet of lined paper.

Direct Teaching-Modeling

Tell students that after writing the summary statement, the second step in summary writing is to create an outline of the specific/key ideas and most significant details in a passage. After asking students to volunteer to read their summary statements from Lesson 6 aloud, write two or three on the board. Then choose one and write it on the display copy of the Key Idea Outline. Next, show students how you would transfer the key ideas from your notes to the outline by copying them next to the keys on the outline (*colors, muscle mass, feed frequently, unique wing movement*).

Then model how you would choose the most significant details that you want to remember for each specific/key idea. For instance, review your notes for the *color* key idea by reading them aloud. Then model your process: "I don't really need to use the Spanish name for hummingbirds because it's in the title and because the key ideas of the article are about the characteristics and behavior of hummingbirds. The difference in color between males and females is strong, so that's a significant detail. I need some additional explanation, but I don't want to list the colors. I'll use *brilliant* and *iridescent* for males and *duller* for females. The words *brilliant* and *iridescent* are precise vocabulary words that help me visualize the many colors of male hummingbirds and *dull* suggests the colors brown and gray. If I use precise vocabulary in the explanations, I'll be able to remember what the most significant details are."

As you begin to add the details to the outline, think aloud about the No More Than 4 rule and point out that you're separating the details with semicolons.

If necessary, continue to model with other paragraphs of notes. As you transition to Stage 2, call on students to tell you which words and phrases from your notes are significant details and how much explanation is needed. Guide them to use precise vocabulary, eliminate lists of examples, and use categorical terms whenever possible.

Materials

* Key Idea Outline reproducible or lined notebook paper (page 96)

* Teacher and student notes and summary statements from Lesson 6

Key Idea Outline

Name _____ Date _____

Summary Statement: _____
_____
_____

Outline:

○—¤ **colors**
  • males brilliant, iridescent; females duller

○—¤ **muscle mass**
  • 30% body weight; 30 m.p.h.; migrate up to 2,000 miles

○—¤ **feed frequently**
  • consume 2/3 of body weight daily; 1,000 flowers; nectar, pollen, insects

○—¤ **unique wing movement**
  • 360° pattern; fly in all directions; backward; hover in midair

Sample Key Idea Outline for "Hummingbirds: Mother Nature's Flying Jewels"

Lesson 8: Writing the Summary Paragraph

Lesson Objective: To write a summary paragraph using the summary statement as the topic sentence and the key idea outline as a guide for the paragraph.

Materials

* Teacher and students' copies of completed Key Idea Outline from Lesson 7

Preparation

Display the copy of your completed Key Idea Outline.

Direct Teaching-Modeling

Share that when we write a summary, the summary statement is the topic sentence. Then we use the summary, or key idea, outline to develop the summary paragraph, writing one or two sentences for each key idea and the most significant details.

Display your completed Key Idea Outline from the previous lesson. Copy the summary statement on a sheet of paper. Then ask yourself, "How can I write these significant details in my outline as sentences?" Compose the next sentence orally, saying, for instance, "The next sentence begins the summary of the key ideas and significant details. It will be about the colors of the birds. Both males and females need to be described because the contrast between them is important. I could write that males and females are different and then add a sentence that describes the difference, but that might be a bit choppy. I think I'll describe the males first: *brilliant, iridescent feathers of many colors* because that includes the key idea as well as some of the details. Next I can describe the females: *duller.* Now I can write a sentence: *The males have brilliant, iridescent feathers of many colors, while the females tend to be duller in color.*"

Compare that sentence to the notes in your outline to ensure that you have included everything. Then continue to the next key idea. Read your notes aloud and comment that there are several significant details, which could make the sentence awkward. Model how you decide to write the key idea in its own sentence and then to combine the three significant details into another sentence. When you've finished writing the sentences, read through your summary paragraph, making any necessary changes and edits.

Finally, remind students that summary paragraphs do not have conclusions, nor should they express an opinion about what you're summarizing.

Small Group Practice: At this point, have students work together to write their summary paragraphs.

"Mother Nature's Flying Jewels," an article by Faye Carter, describes the characteristics and behavior of hummingbirds. The males have brilliant, iridescent feathers of many colors, while the females tend to be duller in color. Hummingbirds have remarkable muscle mass. Their muscles make up 30% of their body weight, making them able to fly 30 m.p.h. and migrate up to 2,000 miles. They must feed frequently and consume 2/3 of their body weight daily. They may visit as many as 1,000 flowers, eating nectar, pollen, and insects. Hummingbirds are the only birds whose wings rotate in a 360° pattern. They can fly in all directions, including backward, and hover in midair.

Summary Paragraph for "Hummingbirds: Mother Nature's Flying Jewels"

Notes From My Classroom

Because of the effectiveness of summary writing in increasing student achievement, I use it on an almost daily basis. I make decisions about how far into the process I want to go by the importance of the content of the day's lessons. I require students to write summary statements about most of the reading selections and lectures. When the content is important for mastery of content standards or for subsequent learning, I have students write a summary statement and create a Key Idea Outline. If the content is essential for mastery of content standards, I ask them to complete the steps by writing a summary paragraph.

Additional Ideas for Summaries

Picture Summaries

After writing the summary statement, students draw pictures to represent the significant details instead of creating a Key Idea Outline.

Note Card Summaries

Students write the summary statement on one side of a note card and the Key Idea Outline on the other.

Movie Guide Summaries

Using the movie summaries found in television guides as models, students write summaries of a passage. I usually begin this strategy by having them write a summary of a fairy tale, such as "The Three Little Pigs." In this strategy, students are writing only the main idea part of the summary statement. This strategy can be used for both expository and narrative passages.

It'll Cost You Summaries

In this game, students have a certain amount of money to spend in the writing of a summary. Words are worth a specific amount, with the articles *a, an, the* being free. The game can be played by having students spend all their money or as little as possible, but they must still write an effective summary. The summary cannot be telegraphic; it must sound like a real sentence. In this strategy, students are writing only the main idea part of the summary statement. For example, if I had one dollar to summarize "The Three Little Pigs," and words were 10 cents each, I might write one of the following: *Pigs build three houses of different materials with different consequences* (spending all my money), or *Effort rewards the doer* (summarizing the moral of the tale and spending little).

Poem Summaries

This strategy was suggested by Jonathan McClure of Jurupa Unified School District. Students write summaries of information in the form of poems, such as haiku, diamante, and acrostic poems. They can illustrate their poems and create a picture summary as well.

Using Summary Writing for the Interpretation of Informational Graphics

Summary writing provides a framework for students to access information in graphics.

✳ The summary sentence states the type of graphic and its purpose.

✳ The Key Idea Outline includes a description of the format of the graphic, several facts represented in it, and an interpretation of trends or conclusions that can be made.

Summary of a Bar Graph

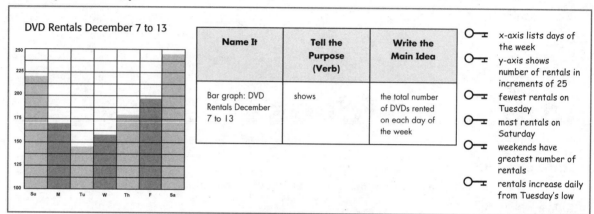

Name It	Tell the Purpose (Verb)	Write the Main Idea
Bar graph: DVD Rentals December 7 to 13	shows	the total number of DVDs rented on each day of the week

- x-axis lists days of the week
- y-axis shows number of rentals in increments of 25
- fewest rentals on Tuesday
- most rentals on Saturday
- weekends have greatest number of rentals
- rentals increase daily from Tuesday's low

Summary of a Diagram

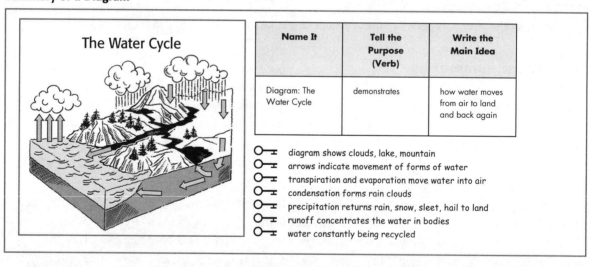

Name It	Tell the Purpose (Verb)	Write the Main Idea
Diagram: The Water Cycle	demonstrates	how water moves from air to land and back again

- diagram shows clouds, lake, mountain
- arrows indicate movement of forms of water
- transpiration and evaporation move water into air
- condensation forms rain clouds
- precipitation returns rain, snow, sleet, hail to land
- runoff concentrates the water in bodies
- water constantly being recycled

Some Final Thoughts

When I began teaching summary writing to my students, I was surprised at the cognitive demands it put on them. A process that seems so simple on the surface requires students to use higher-order thinking skills in an authentic way. Having a step-by-step process helps them master this essential skill.

Often, I have to remind myself that good teaching takes time and persistence. At those times in the process of teaching summary writing, I tell myself that along with note taking, summary writing is the second-most effective teaching strategy for increasing student achievement.

Shapes for Sorting

To the Teacher: Make four copies of this page, each in a different color. Then cut out each shape.

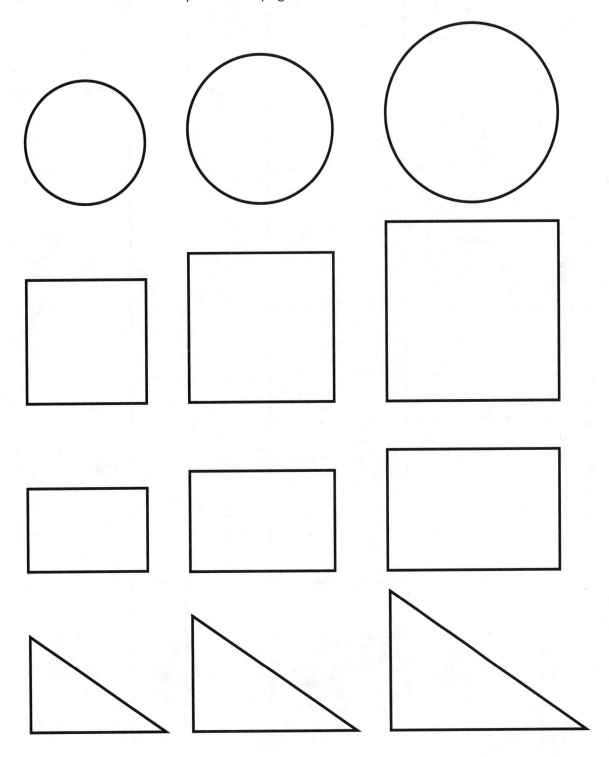

Note Taking Made Easy! © 2010 by Deana Hippie. Scholastic Teaching Resources

Animal Pictures for Classifying

To the Teacher: Make a copy to display to students.

Note Taking Made Easy! © 2010 by Deana Hippie. Scholastic Teaching Resources

T-Chart

T =

Color-Coding:
General ➞ Specific ➞ More/Most Specific Ideas

With your class, decide on a color for each type of idea. Then color each square.

General Idea

The general idea is the largest category.
Each specific idea and more/most specific idea
belongs in this category.

Specific/Key Ideas

Specific ideas (keys) give examples of
the general idea.

More/Most Specific Ideas

More specific ideas (bullets) and most specific
ideas (dashes) give more information about the
specific/key ideas.

Note Taking Made Easy! © 2010 by Deana Hippie. Scholastic Teaching Resources

General ➡ Specific ➡ More/Most Specific

To the Teacher: Each row contains a set of ideas. Cut apart each set.

Idea Sort #1

transportation	two-wheeled vehicle	motorcycle
sports	team	soccer
animal	reptile	lizard
games	board game	chess
school	subject	language arts
family members	female	sister
career	technical	computer repair
clothing	casual	T-shirt
music	popular	oldies
hobbies	collecting	stamps

Note Taking Made Easy! © 2010 by Deana Hippie. Scholastic Teaching Resources

General ➡ Specific ➡ More/Most Specific

To the Teacher: Each row contains a set of ideas. Cut apart each set.

Idea Sort #2

United States	East Coast	West Coast	New York	California
numbers	even	odd	twelve	fifteen
holidays	winter	summer	New Year's Day	Fourth of July
clothing	business	casual	suit coat	sweatshirt
animals	domestic	wild	cows	tigers
food	vegetable	fruit	carrot	apple
amusement parks	rides	attractions	roller coasters	animal shows
transportation	land	sea	train	ship
school	elementary	high school	fourth grade	eleventh grade
technology	communication	entertainment	cell phone	computer game

Note Taking Made Easy! © 2010 by Deana Hippie. Scholastic Teaching Resources

Name _____ Date _____

Recognizing the Structure
of Expository Text

Types of Literature (Model Five-Sentence Paragraph)

Literature can be divided into two basic types. Fiction is one type of literature. Fiction is creative and not based on fact. The second type of literature is nonfiction. Nonfiction is based on facts, details, or opinions.

Healthy Eating (Model Five-Sentence Paragraph)

Healthy eating requires making wise choices. Selecting fruits and vegetables as snacks is a healthy alternative. A crisp apple has few calories, and its crunchiness makes it satisfying to eat. Another wise choice is to rarely eat fast food. Hamburgers, burritos, and pizza, while tasty, are loaded with heart-clogging fat.

The Best Place to Live (Model-Seven Sentence Paragraph)

Most people have a definite preference about where they want to live. Some people prefer to live in large cities. These people enjoy the bustle of city life and the many cultural opportunities. Other people think the suburbs are the ideal place to live. Friendly neighbors and single-family homes attract these people. Another group of people choose to live in more rural areas. The beauty of nature and the solitude draw these people to the countryside.

The Earth Rocks! (Model Eleven-Sentence Paragraph)

The earth is made up of three basic kinds of rocks. One type is igneous rocks. Igneous rocks are created from the liquid core of the earth. Basalt, granite, and quartz are examples of igneous rocks. A second kind is sedimentary rocks. These rocks form from layer upon layer of eroded rock particles deposited on the bottom of lakes and oceans. Limestone, sandstone, and coal are all sedimentary rocks. The third type is metamorphic rocks. When pressure and heat are applied to certain igneous or sedimentary rocks, metamorphic rocks are formed. Very fine-grained rocks like marble, slate, and graphite are examples of metamorphic rocks.

Recognizing Expository Structure in Textbook Passages

Regional Differences in Traditional Native Homes

Northeastern

Tribes in the Northeast lived in forests. They built their homes, known as **longhouses**, in a long, rectangular form with barrel-type roofs. They would tie poles together to form the frame for the house and then cover the frame with bark mats for protection from cold weather. These were multifamily homes with a long hallway in the middle and families' rooms at the sides.

Midwestern Plains

The Plains tribes relied on the buffalo for survival. They did not build permanent homes because they needed to follow buffalo herds as they migrated throughout the year. The Plains tribes built **tipis** in the shape of a cone. The frame was built from long poles fastened together at the top. Animal skins that were fastened to the ground covered the frames. The tipis were easy to erect, take down, and move.

Southwestern

Many Southwestern tribes built multifamily apartment buildings, known as **pueblos**, from dried clay. The adobe bricks provided insulation against the hot temperatures of the summer and the bitter cold of the winter. The pueblos had open areas where the people could gather for ceremonies. When more rooms were needed, they were added on top of the existing ones.

Note Taking Made Easy! © 2010 by Deana Hippie. Scholastic Teaching Resources

Diagram for Recognizing Expository Structure in Textbook Passages

Color each idea in the diagram. Then use the colors to color-code the passage.

General Idea

Specific/Key Idea

More Specific Ideas

Specific/Key Idea

More Specific Ideas

Specific/Key Idea

More Specific Ideas

Regional Differences in Traditional Native Homes

Northeastern

Tribes in the Northeast lived in forests. They built their homes, known as **longhouses**, in a long, rectangular form with barrel-type roofs. They would tie poles together to form the frame for the house and then cover the frame with bark mats for protection from cold weather. These were multifamily homes with a long hallway in the middle and families' rooms at the sides.

Midwestern Plains

The Plains tribes relied on the buffalo for survival. They did not build permanent homes because they needed to follow buffalo herds as they migrated throughout the year. The Plains tribes built **tipis** in the shape of a cone. The frame was built from long poles fastened together at the top. Animal skins that were fastened to the ground covered the frames. The tipis were easy to erect, take down, and move.

Southwestern

Many Southwestern tribes built multifamily apartment buildings, known as **pueblos**, from dried clay. The adobe bricks provided insulation against the hot temperatures of the summer and the bitter cold of the winter. The pueblos had open areas where the people could gather for ceremonies. When more rooms were needed, they were added on top of the existing ones.

Name _____   Date _____

Identifying and Classifying
Informational Words and Phrases

Title: _____

Sentence	Who / What	When / Where	Why / How
1			
2			
3			
4			
5			
6			
7			

Note Taking Made Easy! © 2010 by Deana Hippie. Scholastic Teaching Resources

Name _____   Date _____

The Three Branches of the United States Government

The executive branch is headed by the president with the assistance of the vice president. The executive branch proposes new laws and a budget for the country. As commander-in-chief, the president directs national defense. The president is also responsible for enforcing laws.

The legislative branch is also known as Congress. Congress has two bodies: the House of Representatives and the Senate. Congress has the responsibility of making new laws and passing a budget. Both the House and the Senate must pass new legislation before it becomes law.

The judicial branch is headed by the Supreme Court. The judicial branch is responsible for interpreting the Constitution of the United States and for deciding the constitutionality of laws passed by Congress and state legislatures. The Court's decisions cannot be overturned.

Jigsaw Notes

To the Teacher: Cut out the jigsaw notes on the dashed lines and place in an envelope.

T = Branches of the United States Government

O— executive	— Senate
• president, vice president	• make new laws, pass budget
• proposes new laws, budget	• both house must pass laws, budget
• directs national defense	O— judicial
• enforces laws	• Supreme Court
O— legislative	• interprets the Constitution
• Congress	• decides whether a law is constitutional
— House of Representatives	• decisions cannot be overturned

Note Taking Made Easy! © 2010 by Deana Hippie. Scholastic Teaching Resources

Environmental Adaptations of the Desert Tortoise

The desert tortoise has made many adaptations to its home environment. One adaptation has been to the climatic extremes of the desert. While temperatures can exceed 140° F in the summer, winter temperatures can plunge below freezing. As a result, the desert tortoise builds subterranean burrows and spends 95% of its life in them. The burrows protect the tortoise from the intense heat in the summer and subfreezing temperatures while it is dormant in the winter.

The tortoise has also adapted its diet to this habitat. Grasses, some shrubs, and new growth on cacti along with their flowers make up most of the desert tortoise's diet. When sufficient rainfall causes massive wildflower growth, the tortoise consumes large quantities of the flowers.

Finally, the desert tortoise has adapted to the infrequent rainfall in the desert. The moisture in the grasses and flowers the tortoise consumes makes up most of its water intake. Another source of water is catchment basins that tortoises build in the soil to catch rainfall. They remember the location of the basins and wait near them when rain appears imminent. In addition, an adult tortoise can survive a year without water.

Picture Notes

Title: _____

	•
	•
	•
	•
	•
	•
	•
	•
	•
	•
	•
	•
	•
	•
	•
	•

Note Taking Made Easy! © 2010 by Deana Hippie. Scholastic Teaching Resources

Name _____   Date _____

Two-Pass Notes

Title: _____

1.	
2.	
3.	
4.	
5.	

Note Taking Made Easy! © 2010 by Deana Hippie. Scholastic Teaching Resources

Expository Transitions Bookmark

To the Teacher: Copy this sheet and then cut apart the bookmarks.

Expository Transitions Bookmark	Expository Transitions Bookmark
additionally	additionally
also	also
another	another
finally	finally
first	first
furthermore	furthermore
in addition	in addition
in conclusion	in conclusion
later	later
next	next
one	one
start by	start by
then	then
the second (third, so on)	the second (third, so on)
to begin	to begin
to conclude	to conclude

Note Taking Made Easy! © 2010 by Deana Hippie. Scholastic Teaching Resources

Hummingbirds:
Mother Nature's Flying Jewels
by Faye Carter

Because of their many bright colors, the small birds known as hummingbirds are called *joyas voladoras* in Spanish, or flying jewels. The males have brilliantly colored feathers in many hues, including iridescent reds, greens, pinks, and oranges. The females tend to be duller in color, usually brown or gray.

Hummingbirds have remarkable muscle mass. Their flying muscles make up 30% of their body weight. These large muscle masses make the tiny birds able to fly at speeds of 30 m.p.h. The large muscles are required for migration that can cover up to 2,000 miles from Canada to Panama.

Hummingbirds feed frequently, usually every 10 minutes. They typically consume amounts of food equal to two-thirds of their body weight each day. In its search for food, one bird may visit a thousand flowers in a day to drink their nectar or to eat their pollen. They also feed on gnats, spiders, and sapsuckers. To survive through the night, the hummingbird's metabolism slows dramatically, mimicking hibernation.

Hummingbirds have unique wing movements. They are the only bird whose wings rotate in a 360° pattern. They are the only birds that can fly not only forward but also backward, up and down, and sideways. Because hummingbirds can move their wings in a figure-eight pattern, they can hover in midair, appearing to stay still in space.

Model Paragraphs With Different Purposes

To Provide Relevant Information About a Topic

Bats

Many people think of bats as evil creatures; however, this is not true. Fruit-eating bats help pollinate the flowers of many plants, including wild avocados, guavas, and mangos. As they fly, they also spread the seeds of the fruits they eat in their droppings. Insect-eating bats help control flying insects that spread diseases and damage crops. Scientists study the physics of echolocation—the method bats use to find food—to try to find ways to help blind people use sound waves to move around safely. Other scientists study the saliva of the three species of bats that bite and lick the blood of animals to see if the chemicals in their saliva can control blood clots that can cause

To Narrate a Series of Events

History of the Acoustic Guitar

Guitars developed from variations of the lute and lyre, stringed instruments played by ancient peoples. Early instruments, such as those found in Egypt, Spain, and Asia Minor, had only four strings. In the ninth century, a Persian who lived in Spain is credited with adding a fifth string, which allowed greater musical versatility. Around 1790, a German instrument maker, August Otto, added a sixth string. In the 1800s, the Spanish master instrument-maker Antonio Torres perfected the design of the guitar.

To Compare and Contrast

Athens and Sparta

Both Athens and Sparta were powerful city-states in ancient Greece. For a time, each controlled most of what we now call Greece. Both societies were based on social classes, the lowest being slaves, or helots. Sparta was a dictatorship with a belief in a strong military. Young Spartan boys of the upper classes were taken from their families and trained to be army officers. During the harsh training, they were expected to endure pain without complaint. As adults, Spartans were expected to defend their city to the death. In contrast, Athens is remembered as the birthplace of many Western ideas of democracy and beauty. Young Greek boys of the upper classes were enrolled in academies where they studied history, philosophy, and the arts. As adults, they were expected to share in the government of their city and to make wise decisions.

Note Taking Made Easy! © 2010 by Deana Hippie. Scholastic Teaching Resources

Model Paragraphs With Different Purposes

To Consider Causes and/or Effects

Possible Causes of Declining Amphibian Populations

Amphibian populations, such as frogs, toads, and newts, are declining worldwide. Scientists have suggested several possible causes for the decline. One possibility is the damming of rivers for irrigation and flood control. With less water being released, the swamps and estuaries that amphibians inhabit have dried up or become more saline, or salty. The unregulated use of herbicides and pesticides is another possible cause. The toxins are often washed into the water system. Amphibians have porous skin that permit the poisons to enter their bodies, causing genetic changes or death.

To Describe How to Do a Task or Create a Product

How to Write a Business Letter

When writing a business letter, use a blue or black ink pen and unlined white writing paper or word-process the letter and print it on plain paper. The first step in writing a business letter is to write the heading, including your address and the date in the upper right-hand corner of the paper. After writing the heading, skip down about half an inch and write the name of the recipient and the name and address of the business at the left-hand margin. Now, skip another half an inch and write a salutation such as "Dear Sir or Madam:". Then write the body of the letter using formal language. Be certain to be clear about the purpose of the letter and the action you expect from the company. The last step is to write the closing, followed by a comma, and sign the letter legibly.

Purposes for Expository Writing

General Purpose	Specific Purpose
To inform	To provide information, such as facts, statistics, and descriptions, about a topic
	To narrate a sequence of actual events
	To compare and/or contrast (show similarities and differences) between or among people, places, objects, or ideas
	To consider the causes and/or effects of events or situations
	To describe how to do a task or create a product

Note Taking Made Easy! © 2010 by Deana Hippie. Scholastic Teaching Resources

Sample Lists for Categorization

Schools: preschool, elementary, middle school, high school, college

Wheeled vehicles: car, truck, SUV, bus, tractor, motorcycle

Music genre: classical, rock, hip-hop, heavy metal, jazz, country

Media: newspaper, magazine, television, radio, Internet

Farm animals: cattle, swine, poultry, horses

Big cats: lion, tiger, cougar, leopard, cheetah

Team sports: baseball, basketball, hockey, soccer, football

Civic buildings: school, library, city hall, police station, firehouse

Sciences: biology, physics, chemistry, astronomy, geology

Stages of life: birth, infancy, childhood, teens, adulthood, old age, death

Protozoa: amoeba, slime molds, flagellates, paramecia

States of Matter: solid, liquid, gas

Simple Machines: inclined plane, lever, pulley, wedge, screw, wheel and axle

Western states: California, Arizona, Nevada, Oregon, Washington

Continents: Asia, Europe, North America, South America, Australia, Antarctica

Asian Countries: Japan, China, Laos, Thailand, Vietnam, Tibet

Major World Rivers: Mississippi, Nile, Danube, Ganges, Euphrates, Yangtze

Historical Eras: Middle Ages, Renaissance, Age of Discovery, Industrial Revolution

Ancient Civilizations: Mesopotamia, Egypt, Ancient Greece, Kush, Early India

World Religions: Christianity, Islam, Judaism, Hinduism, Buddhism, Confucianism

American Inventors: Eli Whitney, Robert Fulton, Alexander G. Bell, Thomas A. Edison

Parts of a Plot: exposition, rising action, climax, falling action, resolution

Figurative Language: simile, metaphor, personification, hyperbole

Characterization Techniques: description, dialogue, actions, other characters' opinions

Expository Genre: compare/contrast, process description, definition, analysis, evaluation

Purpose of Sentences: declarative, interrogatory, exclamatory, imperative

Sentence Types: simple, compound, complex, compound-complex

Categorical Terms for
Summary Writing Bookmark

To the Teacher: Copy this sheet and then cut apart the bookmarks.

Categorical Terms

achievements

behaviors

benefits

causes

characteristics

circumstances

consequences

developments

effects

events

ideas

influences

objectives

origins

outcomes

process(es)

purposes

reasons

results

sources

steps (in a process)

traits

uses

Categorical Terms

achievements

behaviors

benefits

causes

characteristics

circumstances

consequences

developments

effects

events

ideas

influences

objectives

origins

outcomes

process(es)

purposes

reasons

results

sources

steps (in a process)

traits

uses

Note Taking Made Easy! © 2010 by Deana Hippie. Scholastic Teaching Resources

Verbs for Summary Writing

Author's Purpose	Verbs for Summary
To provide relevant information about a topic	clarifies, demonstrates, describes, discusses, enumerates, explains, identifies, lists, reveals
To tell about, or narrate, a series of events in chronological order	describes, explains, narrates, recounts, reports, tells
To show similarities and/or differences of people, objects, places, and so on	*similarities:* compares, describes the similarities *differences:* contrasts, differentiates between, distinguishes between
To consider causes for and/or effects of events	describes, proposes, reflects, speculates, surmises, theorizes, traces
To describe how to do a task or create a product	demonstrates, describes, enumerates, explains, identifies, lists, teaches
To influence the reader's opinion or attitude about a topic or issue	attempts to convince, discusses, encourages, endorses, enlists support for, explains, offers reasons, opposes, persuades, presents reasons, proposes, recommends, suggests
To evaluate or make a judgment about an idea, product, process, and so on	analyzes, assesses, condemns, critiques, criticizes, endorses, evaluates, judges, praises, reviews

Learning Preferences
by Jason Evans

Research has shown the presence of three common sensory learning preferences or modalities. Learning modalities are the way people learn and process new information.

Visual learners easily access information through graphic representations, such as charts, pictures, and maps. To learn to do something, they like watching a demonstration. They also are sensitive to formatting in text, using the bullets, headings, and white space to learn and remember information. Visual learners use placement of information on a page to recall the information: the where helps to remember the what.

Auditory learners need to hear and talk about information. They find lecture, discussion, and recitation helpful in learning. People with an auditory preference often write in the same way they speak, so they may have difficulty organizing an essay as they write. Also, they may move their lips while reading silently in order to "hear" the words in their heads.

Kinesthetic learners are grounded in reality and have a distrust of the abstract. They prefer to learn by doing and by trial and error. To learn abstract ideas, kinesthetic learners need real-world examples. They also need to know the "big picture" and understand how everything fits together before they can deal with the details.

Summary

The article "Learning Preferences" by Jason Evans describes the characteristics of the three learning modalities. Visual learners learn by studying graphics and watching demonstrations. Text formatting and the location of information assist them in learning and remembering. Auditory learners need to hear and discuss information. Oral communication is important to them, but organizing writing may be difficult. To "hear" as they read, they may move their lips. Kinesthetic learners are grounded in reality, learning by doing and experimenting. Concrete examples of abstract ideas help them understand. They need to see "big pictures" before they can learn the details.

Note Taking Made Easy! © 2010 by Deana Hippie. Scholastic Teaching Resources

Creating the Summary Statement

Name It	Tell the Purpose (Verb)	Write the Main Idea
Title:		
Author:		
Genre:		

Key Idea Outline

Summary Statement: _____

_____

_____

Outline:

Stephens Elementary
5687 Hwy. 237
Burlington, KY 41005

Note Taking Made Easy! © 2010 by Deana Hippie. Scholastic Teaching Resources